KT-405-497

616.9.

45

ID

CHESHIRE
LIBRARIES

16 JUN 2003

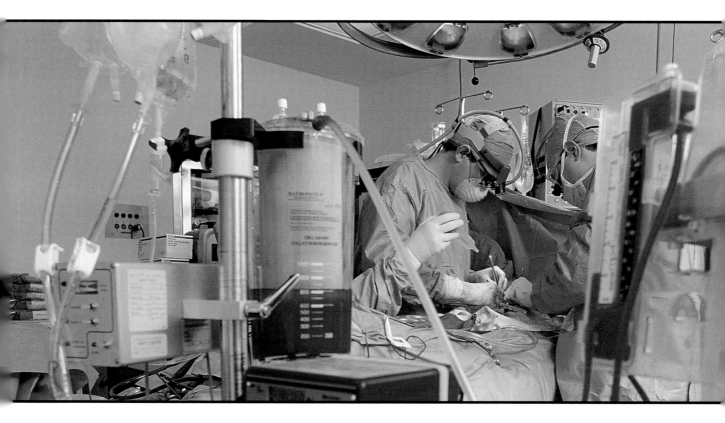

THE CONQUEST OF DISEASE

UNDERSTANDING GLOBAL ISSUES

Published by Smart Apple Media
1980 Lookout Drive
North Mankato, Minnesota 56003
USA

This book is based on *The Conquest of Disease: An impossible dream?*
Copyright ©1998 Understanding Global Issues Ltd., Cheltenham, England.

This edition copyright ©2003, WEIGL EDUCATIONAL PUBLISHERS LIMITED
All rights reserved. No part of this publication may be reproduced, stored in
a retrieval system, or transmitted in any form or by any means, electronic,
mechanical, photocopying, recording, or otherwise, without the prior
written permission of the publisher.

Library of Congress Cataloging-in-Publication Data

The conquest of disease / edited by Jared Keen.
    p. cm. -- (Understanding global issues)
Includes index.
Summary: Examines the occurrence of disease on a global scale and
explores the environmental, social, political, and economic implications
of combating disease.
 ISBN 1-58340-166-0
 1. Medicine--Juvenile literature. 2. Diseases--Juvenile literature.
3. Epidemiology--Juvenile literature. [1. Diseases. 2. Medicine. 3.
Epidemiology.] I. Keen, Jared. II. Series.
 R130.5 C665 2002
 614.4--dc21

                    2001008445

              Printed in Malaysia
              2 4 6 8 9 7 5 3 1

EDITOR Diana Marshall   **COPY EDITOR** Heather Kissock
TEXT ADAPTATION Jared Keen   **DESIGNER** Terry Paulhus
PHOTO RESEARCHER Nicole Bezic King

Contents

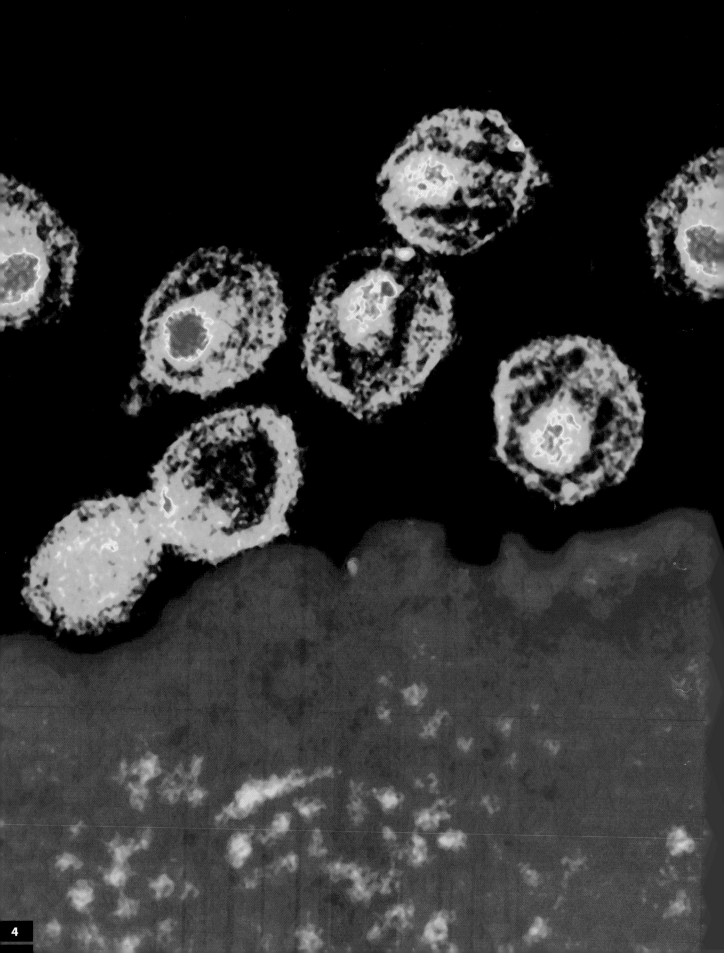

Introduction

During the 1960s, many doctors believed that infectious diseases would soon be conquered. Great advances were being made in the identification and treatment of diseases. Despite the progress, only smallpox has been eliminated. While other common diseases, such as tuberculosis (TB) and malaria, were close to vanishing, they have now returned, stronger than ever before. Some diseases have become resistant to drugs. As science introduces new ways in which to combat disease, it is worth noting that **microbes** possess an extraordinary ability to adapt very quickly to new environments. Many of these microorganisms have been on Earth for billions of years. These age-old organisms can survive in the most hostile conditions and can quickly **mutate** when they experience a change in their environment. **Bacteria** can live along the deepest ocean floor, on the highest mountain summit, in volcanic steam, and even in nuclear power cores. The mortal battle against microbes takes place across the planet.

Since the HIV/AIDS epidemic began, more than 60 million people worldwide have been infected with this highly adaptable virus.

Disease is common in plants, insects, and throughout the animal kingdom. The defeat of one particular form of disease has little impact on the big picture of life on Earth. Since humans share so many **genes** with the plants and animals that surround them, it is never possible to eliminate every disease that might affect them. Jumping from species to species is just one of the many tricks

> *The defeat of one particular form of disease has little impact on the big picture of life on Earth.*

that microbes can perform when necessary. Still, the hope remains that some diseases will eventually be conquered with the use of improved science, increased effort, and more money.

Every year, billions of dollars are spent on health care, the treatment of diseases, and research. However, most medical efforts in today's world continue to focus on the health issues and concerns of paying customers. The fact remains that most of the planet's infectious diseases threaten less developed nations. In addition, the widespread use of commercial drugs has led to a growing resistance to human medicine's only weapon— antibiotics. The progress in modern medicine has brought with it an advancement in the **evolution** of its enemy—disease.

While scientists have made considerable progress in the battle against some diseases, other diseases have proven difficult to combat, or even treat. Several diseases that were once considered mild are now very serious. Combined with growing problems in meeting basic needs, such as sanitation and access to clean water, these diseases now threaten entire populations. There is an urgent need to develop combative approaches to disease on a global level.

With the rise of **globalization** came global disease concerns. As a result of increased travel, diseases that were until recently found only in developing countries have become concerns of developed countries. At the same time, developing countries are beginning to suffer from the diseases once entirely confined to the industrialized world, such as cancer and heart disease. While science is always evolving, so are diseases. Now, in the early part of the 21st century, humans find themselves increasingly involved in a race between science and nature.

Disease and History

Evolution is unforgiving. It severely punishes mistakes. While humankind has shown great ability in shaping the world to suit its needs, its successes have been too small to be meaningful—humans have only had a serious effect on the planet for perhaps 15,000 years. Most of the impact has occurred within the last 200 years. This time frame is a mere blink of the eye when compared to at least 3.5 billion years of

The discovery of the double helix structure, which contains the genetic code, revolutionized DNA research.

microbial history on Earth. It would be foolish to think that humans could win the evolutionary battle with this ancient adversary.

Microbes have had an ongoing effect on Earth's life forms for millions of years.

There has never been a time in history when people lived entirely free of disease. Bacteria, **parasites**, and **viruses** were part of the evolutionary story from the very beginning.

These microbes are so small that humans were unable to detect them until only a few hundred years ago. Still, they have had an ongoing effect on Earth's life forms for millions of years. Many microbes have formed complex relationships with plants and animals—inserting themselves into cells and mixing with **deoxyribonucleic acid (DNA)**. Microbes are as much a part of life as the blood that flows through humans' veins.

Thousands of years ago, humans lived in small groups of hunters and gatherers. They had to cope with infections, parasitic

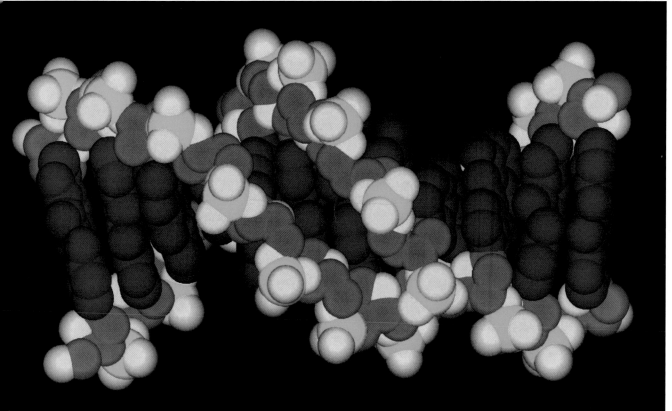

worms, such as tapeworms, inhabiting their digestive systems, and various diseases caught from the animals they hunted. The risk of disease increased with the arrival of agriculture, which brought people into close proximity with cattle, goats, pigs, and poultry. Many common modern diseases originally came from these animals, including smallpox and tuberculosis from cattle; measles from dogs and cattle; influenza (flu) from pigs, ducks, and chickens; and the common cold from horses.

Not until urbanization did the spread of plagues become a reality, causing high mortality rates by the rapid spread of infectious diseases. The crowding of thousands of people in unclean conditions—living alongside rodents, insects, and parasites—provided ideal conditions for the spread of infectious diseases. The rise and fall of many ancient city-based civilizations were often linked to patterns of disease. The plagues that devastated Athens, Greece, in 430 B.C. and Constantinople (now called Istanbul) in A.D. 542 carried fatal consequences for the two great empires. The success of the 16th-century **conquistadors** in Mexico and Peru had less to do with their military strength than with the transfer of new diseases to the local populations, and armies, of the Aztecs and the Incas, which lacked immunity. In 1500, the population of Native Peoples living in North and

The trenches of World War I were a breeding ground for rats, lice, and other vermin.

THE SPANISH FLU

In 1918, a major influenza epidemic marked history. Known as the Spanish flu for its early appearance in that country, it caused eight million deaths in Spain in the month of May. While the flu was nothing new, that year it surfaced with incredible strength, as it does in cycles of 30 to 40 years. The United States had just joined World War I, and the country was prepared for battle. However, they were not prepared for the epidemic that lay ahead. In the summer of 1918, 1.5 million United States soldiers were sent to Europe to fight in the war. Some soldiers carried the flu virus with them on ships across the Atlantic Ocean. With the soldiers living together in such close quarters, the flu quickly spread. Many soldiers died of the flu before ever seeing combat. Those who made it to the front lines brought the disease to the trenches, which were already extremely unsanitary. By November of that year, 21 million people had died worldwide. Between 1918 and 1919, the outbreak spread, infecting one-fifth of the world's population and killing nearly 40 million people. In the United States, the death toll was about 675,000—ten times the number of Americans killed in battle during World War I.

South America was stable, at about 100 million. By 1800, it was less than 10 million. Diseases brought over from other parts of the world spread quickly. The developing world struggles with violent outbreaks and rapid spreads of disease just as most of the world did at the turn of the 20th century. Throughout history, the spread of disease has proven its ability to travel. Today, the possibility that new microbes being transferred from space could have a similar impact on humankind is not entirely without reason.

This painting illustrates the devastation of the French city of Marseilles by bubonic plague in 1720.

AIDS: THE PRESENT-DAY PLAGUE

Many experts are calling the acquired immune deficiency syndrome (AIDS) the present-day plague. While its spread is slower than the plagues of the past, AIDS could prove to be more lethal than its precursors. More than 40 million people worldwide already carry the human immunodeficiency virus (HIV), which causes AIDS. This number is rapidly increasing, especially in Africa and Asia, where prevention programs are poorly funded and drug treatments are too expensive. In 2001, more than 28 million people in Africa were living with AIDS, while approximately 2.3 million died of the disease. In November 2001, the United Nations reported that the number of HIV infections in Eastern Europe was rising faster than anywhere else in the world. The latest figures reveal that more than 75,000 new infections were reported in Russia—an increase of 15 times in just 3 years. There are several factors that contribute to the spread of HIV. High-risk behaviors, such as having unprotected sex or sharing needles, are the main culprits. HIV can also be spread through unsafe or untested blood **transfusions**, and from mother to unborn child. In many countries, blood is now carefully screened with the aim of decreasing the spread of HIV/AIDS. At present, there is no cure for the disease.

BLACK DEATH

The Black Death—so called in England for the black spots it produced on the skin—killed up to one-third of Europe's population. Originating in China, the plague was spread by rat's fleas. Between 1346 and 1350, the Black Death killed 20 million people. Further outbreaks of bubonic plague occurred for centuries to follow. The bacteria responsible for bubonic plague still exist today. Bubonic plague

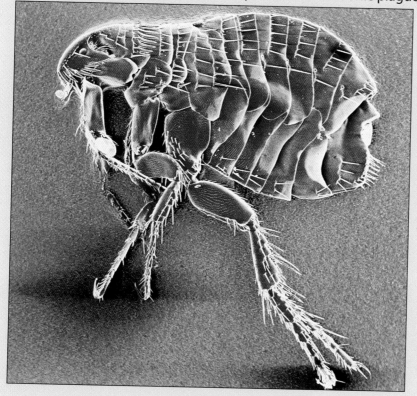

is highly contagious, spreading quickly from person to person via the bacteria in rat's fleas. The first symptoms of illness usually develop within one week of initial infection. Body temperature soars, and pain and confusion follow shortly after. If left untreated, death may occur in two to three days. Occasional outbreaks are reported even today—in the United States, 13 states reported cases between 1984 and 1994.

Throughout history, insects, such as fleas and mosquitoes, have played a major role in the spread of disease.

KEY CONCEPTS

Urbanization People did not always live in cities. While most early peoples lived in rural or country settings, where they hunted or farmed, the trend toward city living began as early as ancient Greece. Urbanization is the process whereby a city or cities gradually develop over time, moving people away from rural communities. People first began to live in close groups as the result of their need for protection, food, and shelter. Certain historical events have contributed to widespread urbanization. The most significant of these was the **Industrial Revolution**. Large factories and processing plants offered many job opportunities, which drew many people into urban centers.

Epidemics Although disease can be found nearly everywhere, outbreaks are usually restricted to particular areas or groups of people. When a disease spreads rapidly, it is called an epidemic. Epidemics can affect towns or parts of cities, continents, or even the world. Most epidemics run their course and then end— either as a result of medical treatment or due to a lack of **hosts**. Some epidemics can take decades to disappear.

Developing Countries Also called the Third World, these countries are economically and technologically less developed than the industrialized world. The Third World is home to two-thirds of the world's population.

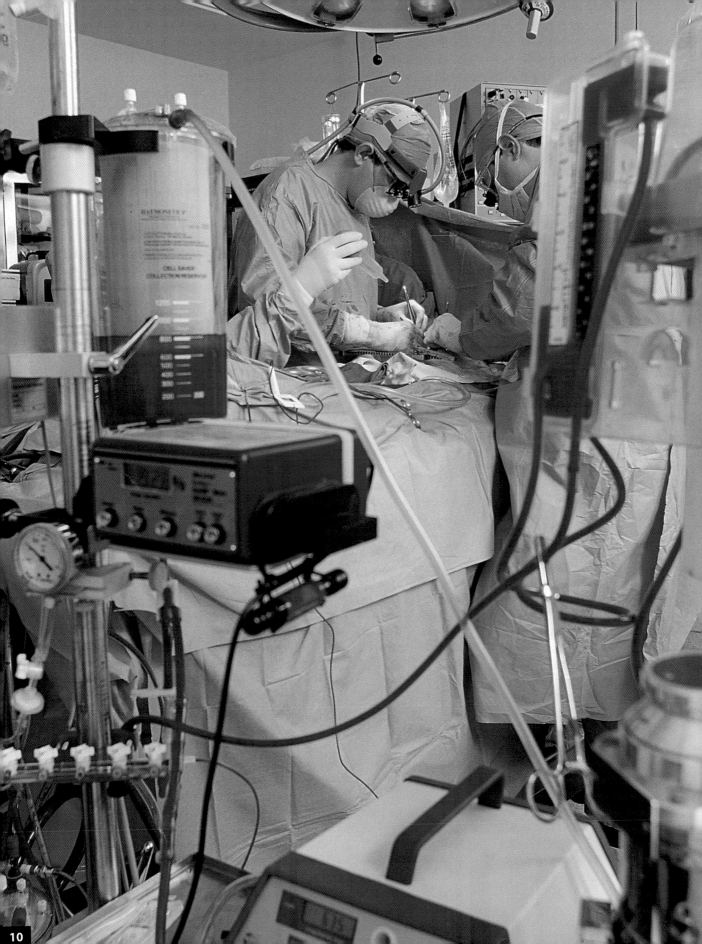

World Health Organization

The World Health Organization (WHO), founded in 1948, is a special agency of the United Nations dedicated to promoting worldwide health. With 191 member nations, the WHO's main objective is the attainment of the highest possible levels of health by all people. In 1996, the main focus of the World Health Organization's annual report was infectious diseases—those that may be passed from person to person by infection or the spread of microbes. These now mostly affect developing countries. On the other hand, the focus of the 1997 report was chronic diseases—those that are long-lasting or recurring—which are most common in the industrialized world. While separating between these two categories is a way of simplifying global disease, the division is not always straightforward or absolute. Infectious viruses and bacteria, for example, can contribute to liver, cervical, and stomach cancers, which are classified as chronic diseases.

Although there are links between infectious and chronic diseases, there are big differences between the health concerns of developed and developing countries. The United States spends billions of dollars on drugs and surgery for citizens who have passed the prime of life, while Africa struggles to keep its children alive amid frequent epidemics.

> *Africa struggles to keep its children alive, while billions of dollars are spent on U.S. citizens past the prime of life.*

The 2001 World Health Report revealed a shift in emphasis—particularly in developed countries—toward researching and understanding mental health, which has long been neglected but is becoming increasingly burdensome. More and more, the wellness of individuals is being closely linked to mental health. This includes coping with infectious diseases, or maintaining the quality of life for those afflicted with chronic disorders.

Throughout the world, more people live longer lives and enjoy better health than ever before. As recently as 1955, the average life expectancy for the world's population was just 48 years. In 1995, it increased to 65 years.

By the year 2025, the global life expectancy is projected to reach 73 years. Just 40 years ago, deaths among children less than 5 years of age numbered about 20 million each year—almost twice today's figure, despite the increase in the number of births. While the world's population in 1955 was less than three billion, today's current population is about six billion.

One result of the increase in life expectancy and global population is that chronic diseases, which at one time were mostly found in Europe and North America, have begun to affect the whole world. As people in developing countries live longer, they also increase their chances of developing chronic disorders, which often afflict the aged.

Developing countries are inheriting the health problems of the developed world. The appearance of lifestyle diseases, which are caused by changes in diet, work, and social activities, in the developing world has given some countries a double threat, since they still battle traditional infectious diseases. Also, several factors that once contributed to good health among rural communities—exercise, fresh air, and low-fat diets—have given way to inactive office jobs, urban pollution, and an unhealthy, fast-food eating

Surgery, a 20th-century development in technology, is not available to many people of the world due to where they live and the high costs of such treatments.

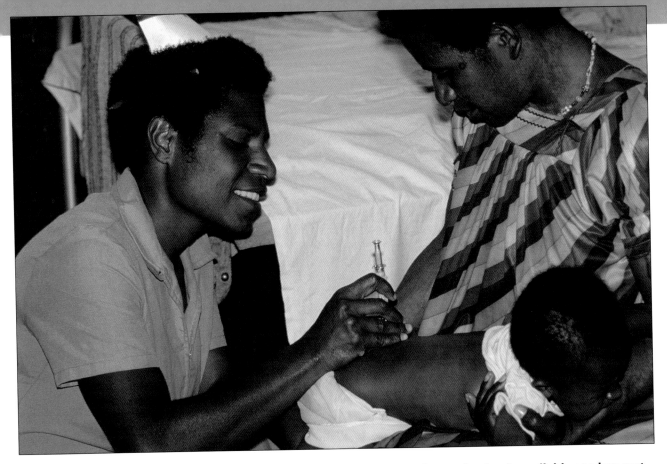

Nearly two million children die each year from diseases for which immunization is available at a low cost.

culture. The increase in cigarette smoking, and alcohol and drug abuse has also added to the strain on health. As a result, the WHO predicts that there will be "global epidemics of cancer and other chronic diseases in the next two decades. The main result will be a huge increase in human suffering and disability."

In addition to the many physical conditions that weaken

KEY CONCEPTS

Immunization Immunization helps the body battle diseases by building immunity, or protection, using vaccines. The vaccines are small quantities of dead or weakened disease organisms, such as viruses and bacteria, that help the body fight disease. A reaction is triggered when a small amount of weakened bacteria is injected into the body. The body's defense systems attack the organism, and the body builds a resistance to the disease. Some vaccines must be administered every few years, while others can provide lifelong protection from particular diseases.

Life Expectancy While all humans eventually die, some will live much longer than others. The length of a person's life is linked to many factors, including behavioral choices, such as drinking alcohol or getting regular exercise; family medical history; and the social, economic, and political conditions in which the person lives. By considering such factors, a person can determine his or her life expectancy. Someone who exercises, eats healthy foods, and lives in a developed country will have a high life expectancy. This means that the individual can be expected to live in good health for as many as 70 years. By contrast, a person who lacks access to clean water or who can trace a family history of disease will have a lower life expectancy.

DISEASES: INFECTIOUS VERSUS CHRONIC

Infectious diseases are transmitted from person to person or location to location through infection. Chronic diseases are not contagious and often develop as the result of aging, lifestyle choices, and environmental factors.

The industrialized world has been able to keep most infectious diseases under control. At the same time, it has seen an increase in a variety of chronic conditions. By contrast, the developing world continues to fall victim to infectious diseases, which consistently claim the lives of millions.

The following are just a few examples of each type:

INFECTIOUS	CHRONIC
• HIV/AIDS	• Alzheimer's disease
• cholera	• arthritis
• malaria	• asthma
• measles	• cancer
• pneumonia	• diabetes
• tuberculosis	• heart disease

human health, **mood disorders**, including depression, affect about 450 million people at any given time. About 45 million people worldwide suffer from schizophrenia, a mental disorder characterized by delusions and confusion. The United States spends more on drugs for **nervous system disorders**— about $3.2 billion is spent annually on the treatment of schizophrenia alone—than for any other health condition.

Following the WHO's worldwide immunization program, the eradication of smallpox in 1977 confirmed the great need for global political health efforts. Immunization programs currently protect about 80 percent of the world's children from six major childhood illnesses—diphtheria, measles, polio, tetanus, tuberculosis, and whooping cough. Unfortunately, many of these children do not have access to clean water and nutritious foods that are essential for staying healthy.

Regular exercise promotes both physical and psychological health.

While the defeat of malaria remains a distant goal, the WHO hopes to eliminate a number of other serious diseases. These include polio, which is already down to fewer than 100,000 cases worldwide; guinea worm, a parasite that lives under the skin; leprosy; Chagas disease; river blindness; and elephantiasis. As part of this eradication process, some pharmaceutical companies

Car exhaust contains harmful chemicals, such as carbon monoxide and nitrogen dioxide. These chemicals have been linked to cancers, nerve damage, asthma, and various other respiratory diseases.

have spent the last decade implementing aid programs for developing countries. The United States firm, Merck and Company, has been donating the drug ivermectin to treat river blindness in Africa and South America. Another pharmaceutical research giant, SmithKline Beecham (now half of GlaxoSmithKline), is currently providing billions of free doses of the drug albendazole, helping the WHO in its efforts to wipe out elephantiasis over the next two decades. The company is committed to a 20-year program that will cost up to $1.7 billion to run.

In the developed world, people are much healthier than they used to be. Life expectancies have risen, and fewer people suffer from **debilitating** diseases, such as muscle disorders. Still, large numbers of people complain about aches, pains, fatigue, and depression. In the United States, the Public Health Service spends more money on health services and research every year, despite the fact that many of the diseases that were once common have since been defeated or controlled. This inconsistency is only partly explained by the aging of the population. The developed world is full of people searching for signs of sickness even when they are healthy, well-fed, comfortable, and insect-free.

These feelings are often justifiable, as the line dividing health and disease is becoming less and less distinct. Many past infectious diseases—from cholera to tuberculosis—have resurfaced in recent years, showing new strength and high levels of drug resistance. At least 30 dangerous new diseases have been identified in the last two decades. Some experts blame environmental pollution for these health developments. Others have argued that the return of diseases is the natural response of viruses and bacteria to human progress, in the never-ending war of evolution between humans and microbes.

Duties: Studies the spread and origin of diseases

Education: Master's degree in epidemiology, public health, or other related specialty

Interests: Public health and its environmental and biological influences, research techniques, and problem solving

Navigate to the Public Health Careers Web site: www.publichealthjobs.com for information on related careers. Also, click on www.cdc.gov/epo/dapht/eis/ for more information about epidemiology jobs.

Careers in Focus

Epidemiologists are public health specialists who research and study the origins, causes, and spread of diseases within a population. These scientists solve the mysteries of disease by tracing the development of the characteristics of a particular disease, including lifestyle practices, environmental conditions, treatment effects, and risk factors. The goal of epidemiological research is to aid in disease treatment and prevention through the mapping out of diseases.

Epidemiologists may work in laboratories, where they examine and analyze bacteria or viruses in blood samples, or they may conduct fieldwork in locations where diseases appear. Fieldwork often involves interviewing those who have fallen ill to determine possible factors that influence the appearance of a disease in a particular population or geographical region. While several of the epidemiological studies involve the observation of the conditions that facilitate the spread or outbreak of infectious diseases—such as malaria or TB—others analyze the risk factors that promote chronic diseases, including cancer and heart disease. The connection made between smoking and lung cancer was the result of epidemiological work from around the world. The causes of epidemics or unusual outbreaks have also been determined by epidemiologists. The cause of the 1993 *Escherichia coli* 0157:H7 (*E. coli*) outbreak—which infected 500 residents from Washington, Idaho, California, and Nevada—was traced back to its cause, undercooked meat, by epidemiologists. They work alongside local and international public health organizations, physicians, government agencies, and research facilities to understand and control disease.

Infectious Diseases

Until the 1940s, infectious diseases were as much a problem for developed nations as they were for tropical Africa. European and North American children often died of scarlet fever, diphtheria, measles, whooping cough, smallpox, and a number of other illnesses. Premature deaths in families were commonplace. In fact, since 16.5 percent of the world's children could be expected to die within the first few years of life, women in the early 1900s often had large families. Doctors were slow to recognize the causes of disease. Cholera and typhus were

---

It took many years to convince doctors of the existence of disease-carrying germs.

---

thought to exist in unclean air. It took chemists Louis Pasteur and Robert Koch many years to convince doctors of the existence of disease-carrying **germs**. Surgeons often performed operations without washing their hands between operations or changing their blood-soaked aprons. Antiseptic agents, or cleaners, that destroy germs were rarely used.

Today, microscopes clearly show the bacteria, viruses, and parasites that share the world with humankind. They live in, on, and around people in the trillions. Invisible to the naked eye, they perform many important functions in the human body, and in the wider biosphere. While their role in causing disease is unquestioned, the exact ways in which they do so are often hard to identify.

Malaria has been one of the most troublesome diseases in human history. Common in 91 countries, malaria puts 40 percent of the world's population at risk. Global warming could soon increase that figure to 60 percent as the malaria zone, the area within which the *Anopheles* mosquito thrives, expands. Each year, there are between 300 million and 500 million cases of malaria worldwide, causing more than 2 million deaths, mostly among African children. Of those who survive, many become extremely weak. In the 1950s, it was widely believed that malaria could be

TUBERCULOSIS: THE KILLER VIRUS

In 1993, the WHO declared a global emergency over tuberculosis (TB), warning that 30 million deaths could occur by 2000 unless drastic measures were taken. Today, two million deaths occur each year, causing previous estimations to be revised. The WHO now predicts that between 2000 and 2020, nearly 1 billion people will become newly infected, 200 million will become ill, and 35 million will die, if TB is not effectively controlled. Although 95 percent of TB sufferers are from the developing world, tuberculosis cases are rising in the United States and Europe. Often in lethal combination with HIV, tuberculosis kills many AIDS sufferers. Since AIDS affects the body's **immune system**, it leaves the body weakened and unable to fight off infections. Tuberculosis is particularly deadly in this instance. While one-third of the world's population is infected with TB, only a small percentage ever goes on to develop the disease. The BCG vaccine, developed in the 1920s, yielded its first effective treatment in 1944. Since then, TB has demonstrated an increase in resistance to drugs—a frightening prospect for one-third of the world's population.

stamped out with a combination of insecticides aimed at the mosquito carrier and human immunizations. Now, more than 50 years later, malaria still thrives—due largely to the adaptability of the mosquito. The female *Anopheles* mosquito lands on a human or animal and pierces the skin to get its meal of blood. As it does so, it injects parasites into the bloodstream of the host. Once inside the host's body, the parasites travel to the liver, and then to red blood cells, causing a variety of unpleasant symptoms—from headaches and fever to kidney failure and seizures—and sometimes death. Efforts to completely destroy malaria have been successful in

---

Malaria still thrives, due largely to the adaptability of the mosquito.

European countries, such as Denmark and Great Britain. In the tropics, conquering malaria has proven problematic, except in highly industrialized areas, such as Singapore. The usual technique has involved a combination of draining the marshes where the mosquitoes lay their eggs, killing any survivors with insecticides, and supplying drugs to the local population to kill any parasites in their blood. In the tropics, a large number of breeding sites, from irrigation ditches to discarded plastic bags, make eliminating mosquitoes nearly impossible. While

Without an effective malaria vaccine, the *Anopheles* mosquito remains one of the world's most dangerous killers.

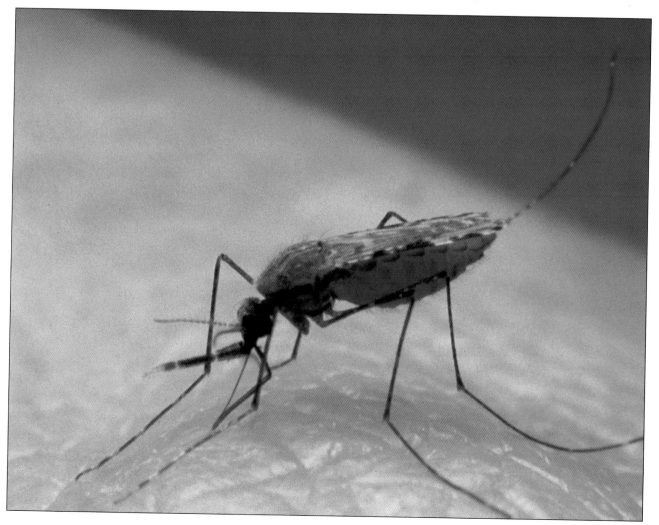

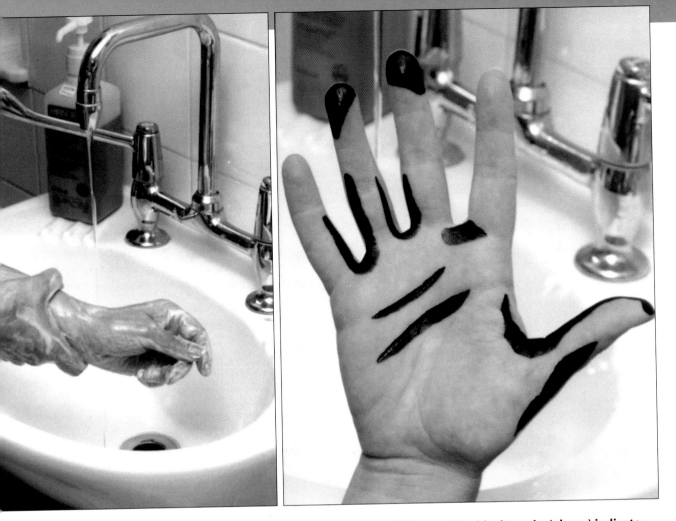

Clean hands are important in the prevention of the spread of disease. The black marks (above) indicate areas commonly missed when washing hands.

draining marshes can be very effective, spraying with insecticides has resulted in the creation of mosquitoes that are resistant to toxins.

Other diseases carried by mosquitoes include yellow fever, dengue fever, encephalitis, elephantiasis, and Rift Valley Fever (RVF). About 1.1 billion people in Africa, Asia, and Latin America are at risk from elephantiasis, which is caused by parasitic worms in the human **lymphatic system**. Still, the most common infectious diseases are those carried in water and sewage. They range from cholera to amoebic dysentery. Water is the ideal medium for microbes, since every animal has to drink water to survive. Humans are also in regular contact with water through washing and farm irrigation. Keeping water free of contamination is the

KEY CONCEPTS

Parasites Parasites are organisms that live in or on other plants or animals for food. Parasites include ticks and certain types of worms and fungi. Tapeworms, which can be caught from eating infected meat, are fairly common parasites in humans. Once inside the host, the tapeworm attaches itself to the host's intestines. There, it lives off the food that the host eats, depriving the host of nourishment. Tapeworms can weaken immune systems and cause weight loss, or even death.

Sanitation Sanitation involves controlling the environment to

most effective way to protect human health, followed closely by providing proper sanitation. These two basic needs persuaded the United Nations (UN) to launch a 10-year campaign to provide clean drinking water and sanitation to everyone in the world by 1990. Although great progress was made, that date has long since passed, and there are still more than one billion people without either safe water or proper sanitation. In countries that provide these basic services, far lower rates of disease have been reported.

The water-borne cholera has experienced a revival in recent years, beginning with a major outbreak in Peru in 1991. The disease broke out along the coast, spreading through the country within the first two weeks. Within one year, it had spread to 11 countries, reaching out across the entire South-American continent. Between 1991 and 1995, 1.34 million cholera cases were reported in North and South America. The epidemic claimed 11,338 lives during this period. In 1992, India experienced the next major cholera epidemic, in which many more lives were lost. In the early years of the 21st century, Africa continues to battle frequent outbreaks of the disease, which spreads from district to district, killing hundreds each year. Since cholera has been a major disease for centuries, it is fairly easy to diagnose and treat. However, it has not proven simple to deal with the range of new diseases that has appeared in recent years, including Lyme disease, legionnaires' disease, hantavirus, and the Ebola virus.

The deadly Ebola virus has appeared sporadically since its initial identification near the Ebola River in 1976.

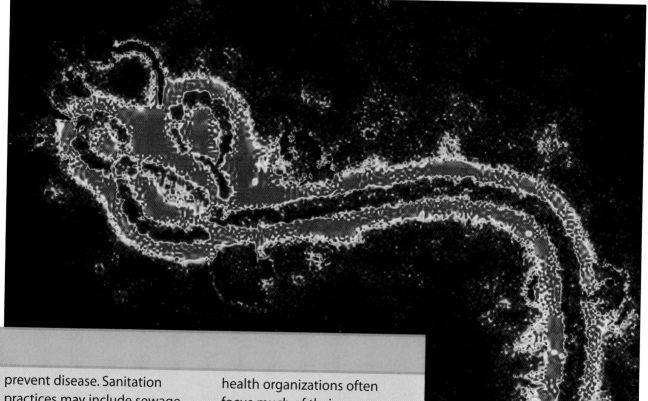

prevent disease. Sanitation practices may include sewage treatment, personal cleanliness, or surgical precautions. Disease-causing microbes thrive in unsanitary conditions. As a result, health organizations often focus much of their resources on sanitation efforts. The cleaner the living environment, the less likely it is to contain infectious organisms.

DISEASE AS WARFARE

In the summer of 1990, the president of Iraq, Saddam Hussein, invaded neighboring Kuwait against UN directives. The Persian Gulf War began in August 1990. The UN's attempt to prevent Hussein from developing biological weapons as retaliation has focused attention on another aspect of disease—the deliberate spread of bacteria or viruses as a method of destroying one's enemies. While biological weapons were outlawed by the Biological Weapons Convention of 1972, the UN has struggled to enforce the agreement, and there is little doubt that some countries have continued to research and develop biological weapons. For a developing but ambitious nation, biological weapons have clear value. They are relatively easy and inexpensive to make, easy to hide, and easy to use. It is not necessary to develop complicated weapons—common anthrax will kill almost anyone who breathes its spores, unless they have been treated with vaccines or antibiotics. Unlike conventional weapons, such as guns and missiles, diseases kill humans, while leaving buildings and other physical assets intact.

Anthrax, one of the oldest known diseases, has in recent years been used as a weapon of war. The worst outbreak of anthrax occurred in 1979, in Sverdlovsk, Russia (present-day Yekaterinburg), when a biological weapons plant accidentally released anthrax spores, killing 66 people. Following laboratory results, American scientists were able to determine that at least four different strains of anthrax had been released by the spores. The accident raised concerns that new, vaccine-resistant forms of anthrax were being developed as biological weapons.

During the months following the devastating terrorist attack on the World Trade Center in New York City on September 11, 2001, cases of inhaled anthrax—the most deadly form of the disease—were reported in the United States. Several deaths across the country, as well as anthrax infections and scares worldwide, resulted in the involvement of the United States' Federal Bureau of Investigation (FBI). The use of microorganisms or toxins from living organisms to produce disease or death in humans, plants, or animals—biological terrorism—was the primary concern.

The WHO estimates that only 110 pounds (50 kg) of *Bacillus anthracis* spores, with airborne distribution, could kill or incapacitate about half of the population of any major metropolitan area. With easy access and relatively low cost, biological agents, such as anthrax, could become the 21st century's plagues. Although the United States is by far the strongest country in terms of conventional weapons, even it is vulnerable to biological warfare. The risk to Europe and Japan, with their higher population densities, is even greater.

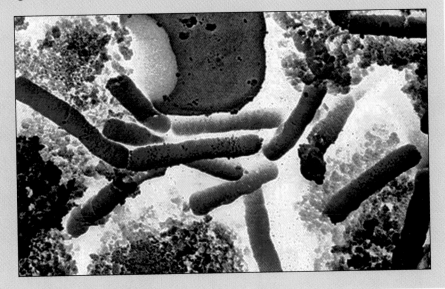

■ Anthrax is a spore-forming bacterium. Since these spores have protective coats, they can withstand extreme conditions, such as heat and drought. This ability to survive makes anthrax spores ideal biological weapons.

Biography
Louis Pasteur

Born: December 27, 1822, in Dole, France
Died: September 28, 1895, in Saint-Cloud, France
Legacy: Uncovered the nature of infectious disease, invented pasteurization, and helped develop the first vaccine

Navigate to the Epidemic Discoveries Web site: www.discovery.com/exp/ epidemic/epidemic.html for information on related milestones in disease. Also click on www.cdc.gov/ for more information about vaccination.

People in Focus

Louis Pasteur was a world-renowned French chemist and biologist who founded the science of microbiology. Earning a doctorate at the École Normale Supérieure in Paris, with a focus on physics and chemistry, Louis Pasteur spent several years applying science to practical problems. Devoting himself to research, Pasteur used France's alcohol manufacturing industry to uncover the process of **fermentation**. He observed that the desired result relied on yeast, and that the souring of alcohol was due largely to additional organisms, such as bacteria. Solving a major economic problem in the process, Pasteur revealed the presence of microorganisms in nature. Eventually, the processes of fermentation and **pasteurization** led Pasteur to conclude that germs were introduced from the environment. This disproved the assumption of the time that bacteria simply appeared spontaneously.

In 1865, while researching a disease in silkworms that had been decreasing the country's production of silk, Pasteur proved that disease could be contagious and hereditary. This led to the germ theory of disease, confirming his belief that the origin and development of disease is comparable to the origin and process of fermentation. Disease, therefore, comes from the germs that attack the body.

In the 1870s, Pasteur's research on anthrax, a fatal disease found in cattle, led to a discovery: introducing the body to a mild form of a particular bacterium builds natural immunity in defense against potential bacterial attacks. Pasteur's early research led modern medicine to the practice of vaccination in the prevention of disease.

Chronic Diseases

Whereas an infectious disease strikes fear in entire communities, the direct impact of a chronic disease, such as cancer or Alzheimer's disease, affects mainly the individual. This is because it is not communicable.

Since its invention in the 1950s, the cardiac pacemaker has saved millions of lives in the developed world, where chronic heart disorders are most common.

Cancer is a disease that still strikes fear in the hearts of those who develop it, even though the cure rate is now far better than that of only a decade ago. Cancer is the leading cause of death in Canada, and is second only to heart disease in the United States. Certain cancers can usually be cured if diagnosed early enough. As people live longer, problems with human mechanics, or functions, increase. The body parts begin to

deteriorate, or break down, resulting in a variety of disorders, such as heart failure, breathing difficulties, and arthritis. Many residents of developed nations who live beyond the age of 70 years can expect heart surgery or the replacement of a hip or knee joint. The replacement of body parts has become a thriving industry in response to the growing demand from an aging population. Diseases of aging

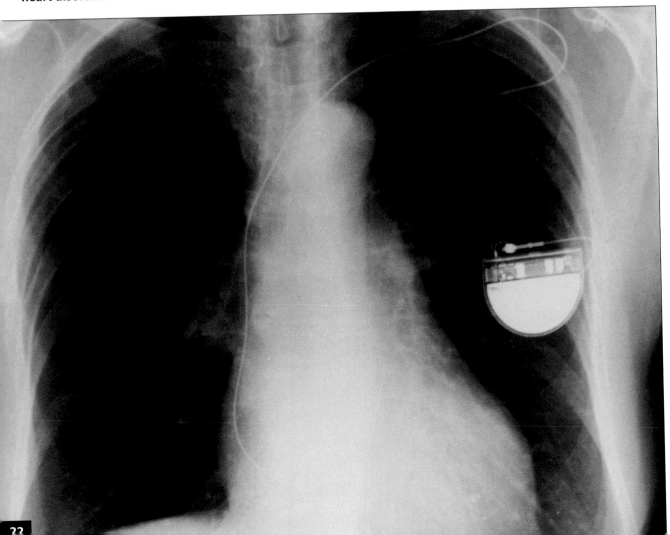

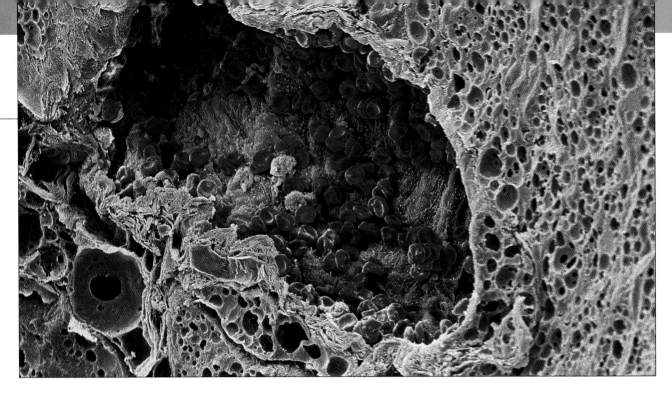

also include the degeneration of the brain in conditions such as Alzheimer's disease. These diseases were once rare in the developing world, simply because few people survived long enough for the diseases to develop. This situation is changing rapidly. By 2025, more than 80 million people in Africa, Asia, and Latin America are expected to suffer from various forms of senile dementia, including all forms of memory loss and confusion that can accompany old age.

Health and diet are closely linked. As such, the health of each individual influences his or her risk of developing a chronic

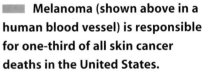 **Melanoma (shown above in a human blood vessel) is responsible for one-third of all skin cancer deaths in the United States.**

disease. Although at least one billion people across the planet are malnourished, obesity is a growing problem throughout the developed world. One in three Americans is clinically obese, while 55 percent of its adult population is considered overweight by international

KILLER CHRONIC DISEASES OF THE WORLD

Chronic diseases are responsible for millions of deaths around the world. This chart shows the chronic diseases that claimed the most lives in 2000.

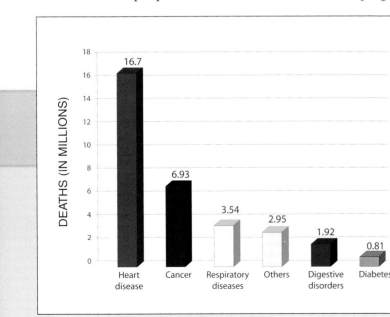

DEATHS (IN MILLIONS)

- Heart disease: 16.7
- Cancer: 6.93
- Respiratory diseases: 3.54
- Others: 2.95
- Digestive disorders: 1.92
- Diabetes: 0.81

standards. Obesity has doubled in the United Kingdom since 1980, affecting about 15 percent of the population. Obesity in children is especially dangerous, since it often results in future health problems, such as high blood pressure and heart attacks. The rapid growth of convenience foods, such as hamburgers and prepackaged meals, in developing-world diets has contributed to a growing crisis in developing countries also. The typical industrialized-world diet contains high levels of sugar and saturated fat—nearly twice the level recommended by the WHO for the maintenance of good health. The American Cancer Society has linked one-third of all cancers in the United States to a high-fat diet.

Americans also suffer heart disease at much higher rates than Greeks or southern Italians. This is largely due to their Mediterranean-style diets.

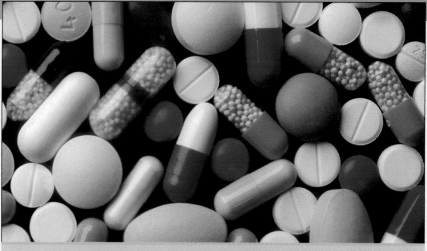

PREVENTION IS BETTER THAN CURE—BUT LESS PROFITABLE

More than $25 billion is spent on drug research each year, most of it on the chronic diseases common in industrialized countries. The free market does not conduct large-scale research into the medical problems of developing countries, whose citizens cannot afford to pay for new drugs. Most large pharmaceutical companies strongly resist the idea of selling cheap, generic drugs in the developing world, arguing that this practice discourages innovation. About 95 percent of health-care spending in the United States is on medical treatment rather than on disease prevention, even though preventing disease is far more cost effective. The $1 spent on a vaccine typically saves more than $20 in avoided health-care costs. The World Health Organization (WHO) estimates that eradicating polio would save the world $3 billion each year by 2015.

KEY CONCEPTS

Smoking Smoking has been linked to many health problems, including cancers, strokes, and emphysema. People who smoke heavily have considerably lower life expectancies than those who do not smoke at all. Billions of dollars are spent each year in the treatment of smoking-related health problems. However, the tobacco industry generates billions of dollars every year, and governments gain revenues from taxing items, such as cigarettes.

Human Impact The strain that human progress has placed on the environment has been enormous. In many ways, humankind has contributed to spreading the very diseases that it is desperately trying to conquer. Changes in the environment cause changes in the organisms living within it. As a result, environmental responsibility has become a necessary strategy in the battle against disease. Canadian research is currently linking many environmental contaminants to the increase in childhood diseases. Childhood cases of asthma, which have increased to four times the number seen 20 years ago, and childhood cancers, which have increased 25 percent in 25 years, are confirming environmental links to disease. Efforts made now to protect the environment may lower future incidence of disease.

DISEASES AND THE ENVIRONMENT

The last 100 years have seen massive increases in the impact of humans on the planet. Of these changes, some that are likely to have a corresponding impact on disease include:

Deforestation: The loss of habitat associated with large-scale removal of trees has forced microbes to switch from animal to human hosts, who have much less resistance to parasites.

Megacities: More people are living in cities than ever before. Health problems present themselves when, in some cases, large numbers of undernourished people live in rodent-filled cities that lack clean water or sanitation.

Pollution: Each year, millions of tons of toxic materials and untreated sewage are released into the air, buried under sand, or dumped into seas. This affects our air quality, water supplies, and land fertility by providing ideal breeding conditions for viruses, bacteria, rodents, insects, and harmful algae.

Globalization of food supply: Many food products are shipped all over the world, increasing the risk of food-borne diseases spreading across the planet.

Mass migration and tourism: Every year, hundreds of millions of people cross international borders for work or travel. This greatly increases the opportunities for bacteria, viruses, and parasites to reach new, and perhaps more vulnerable, populations.

Chemicals: The manufacture and release of thousands of new chemicals into the environment may damage human immune and reproductive systems, or trigger unwanted genetic mutations in both humans and microbes.

Global warming: Insect and microbial activity increases with rises in temperature. Any extension of tropical regions, northward or southward, will result in an increase in warm-climate diseases, such as malaria.

Including pure olive oil, garlic, and plenty of fresh vegetables and fruits, Mediterranean diets are much healthier. With such increasing numbers of chronic disease sufferers, the WHO believes that heart disease and depression will soon replace respiratory infections and diarrheal diseases as the main causes of death and disability worldwide.

One of the most dangerous potential health problems of the future lies in the huge number of new smokers in the developing world. Since only 7 percent of women in the developing world smoke—compared to 24 percent in the developed world—there is great potential for increased cigarette sales in countries in Asia and Latin America. Worldwide, more than one billion people smoke, and one-third of them are likely to die from smoking-related diseases as a result. A number of chronic illnesses have been linked to smoking, from chronic bronchitis to lung cancer. The WHO believes that by 2020, there will be about 10 million tobacco-related deaths each year, of which 70 percent will be in developing countries. While the health risks of smoking are well publicized in the developed world, smoking is still advertised as a glamorous activity in Asia and other parts of the developing world. Taxes on tobacco provide a large portion of government revenue in many countries—yet smoking-related disease costs even more. In China, revenue

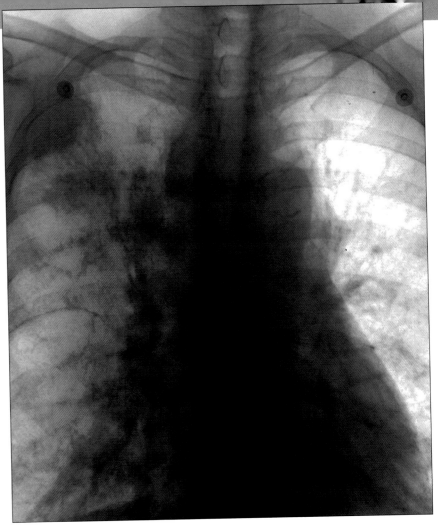

from tobacco taxes in 1999 was $11.92 billion, while health-care and loss-of-productivity costs were about twice that figure. Recent studies have shown that China will soon have the highest death rate from smoking.

> *One of the most dangerous health problems of the future lies in the huge number of smokers.*

Already, close to 1.2 million deaths each year are attributed to smoking and smoking-related diseases. The issue of smoking raises the uneasy choice between

In the United States, nearly 90 percent of all lung cancer cases (highlighted in pink above) occur in people who are or once were smokers.

individual freedom and government responsibility for health care. The solution adopted by the developed world was to put high taxes on tobacco and to restrict advertising and sports sponsorship. This practice has not yet been applied in developing countries, which spend far less on health care than developed countries. After all, tobacco taxes provide a much-needed source of income to many governments.

Duties: Assesses the symptoms of patients together with diet and lifestyle factors, and prescribes drugs or medical treatment according to the diagnosis

Education: Premedical bachelor's degree in science, followed by medical school

Interests: Health care, medicine, and patient care

Navigate to the Careers in Medicine Web site: www.aamc.org/students/considering/careers.htm for information on related careers. Also, click on www.studentdoctor.net/index.asp for more information about physician jobs.

Careers in Focus

A physician, or doctor, can specialize in many different areas, including general practice or family medicine, heart disease, internal medicine, child care, or cancer treatment. All physicians, regardless of specialty, are responsible for the assessment, treatment, and prevention of disease. A physician can diagnose the presence of disease by considering a patient's health; physical history; lifestyle habits, such as fitness and stress; symptoms; and examination results. Physicians use a variety of technological tools, such as blood tests and x-rays, to help diagnose disease. Once a disease is diagnosed, physicians prescribe medications or treatments to alleviate symptoms or to cure the disease. While most symptoms are treatable, many diseases exist for which there are no cures. Some treatments involve altering lifestyle habits, including reducing fat content in an individual's diet or prescribing an increase in exercise. Physicians also provide information on the prevention of chronic diseases. A physician might suggest to a patient who complains of shortness of breath and coughing that they quit smoking cigarettes, in order to treat current symptoms and reduce the risk of lung cancer.

Doctors must stay informed of the constant new discoveries made in the medical sciences. These affect the ways in which medicines are prescribed and alter the techniques and methods used in the detection and diagnosis of disease. A physician is always learning.

Physicians are specialists in disease, both infectious and chronic, and in the microorganisms that cause it.

Mapping Global Disease

Figure 1: Discovering New Diseases

Approximately 30 new diseases have been identified since 1976. The concentration of new diseases in the U.S. is partly attributed to the country's high levels of scientific investigation. It is possible to identify the areas where outbreaks are most likely to occur. The biodiversity of rainforests makes them particularly rich in microbes, while deforestation forces a microbial jump toward human hosts. Urban centers are the other likely areas for disease outbreaks, as crowds and transportation increase microbial travel.

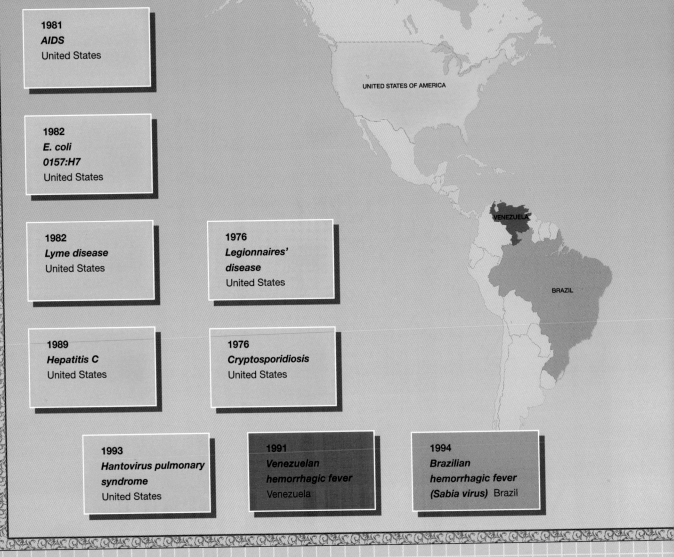

1981
AIDS
United States

1982
E. coli
0157:H7
United States

1982
Lyme disease
United States

1976
Legionnaires'
disease
United States

1989
Hepatitis C
United States

1976
Cryptosporidiosis
United States

1993
Hantovirus pulmonary
syndrome
United States

1991
Venezuelan
hemorrhagic fever
Venezuela

1994
Brazilian
hemorrhagic fever
(Sabia virus) Brazil

UNITED STATES OF AMERICA

VENEZUELA

BRAZIL

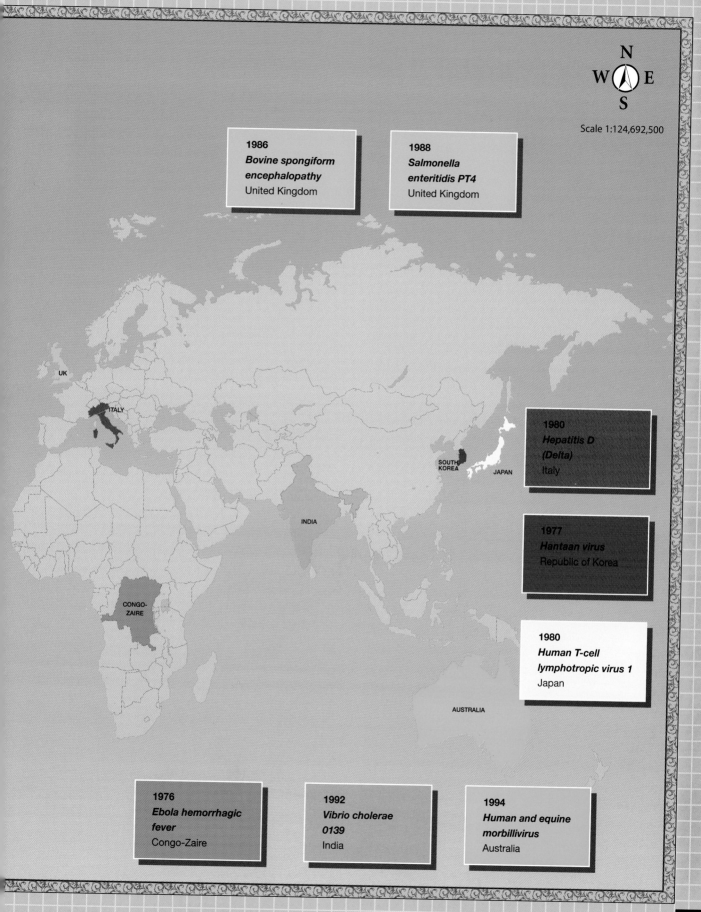

1986
Bovine spongiform encephalopathy
United Kingdom

1988
Salmonella enteritidis PT4
United Kingdom

Scale 1:124,692,500

1980
Hepatitis D (Delta)
Italy

1977
Hantaan virus
Republic of Korea

1980
Human T-cell lymphotropic virus 1
Japan

UK

ITALY

SOUTH KOREA

JAPAN

INDIA

CONGO-ZAIRE

AUSTRALIA

1976
Ebola hemorrhagic fever
Congo-Zaire

1992
Vibrio cholerae 0139
India

1994
Human and equine morbillivirus
Australia

Charting Disease

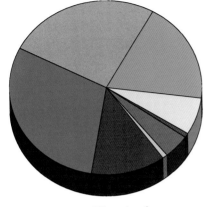

55.7 million deaths

Figure 2: Causes of Death (2001)

Infectious and parasitic diseases continue to be the main killers in developing countries, while heart disease claims the most victims in the developed world. Despite the fact that immunization, safe food and water, and proper sanitation help to protect the developed world from infectious diseases, travel and global warming are increasing their spread.

■ Cardiovascular diseases 30.0%
■ Other or unknown causes 25.6%
■ Infectious and parasitic diseases 18.8%
■ Cancer 12.4%

□ Respiratory infections 7.1%
■ Perinatal conditions 4.4%
■ Maternal or pregnancy related conditions 0.9%
□ Nutritional deficiencies 0.8%

Figure 3: World's Top Ten Killers (2000)

Cases of cancer and heart disease are on the rise in the developed world, while malaria is beginning to spread to regions previously unaffected by the disease. As global warming increases, the malarial zone expands north and south. The use of antibiotics is increasing resistant strains of diseases, such as tuberculosis, which has made a comeback.

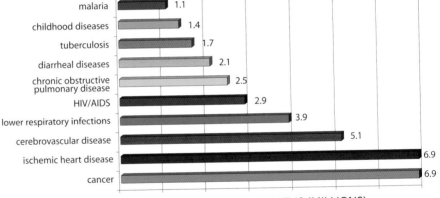

	APPROXIMATE ANNUAL DEATHS (MILLIONS)
malaria	1.1
childhood diseases	1.4
tuberculosis	1.7
diarrheal diseases	2.1
chronic obstructive pulmonary disease	2.5
HIV/AIDS	2.9
lower respiratory infections	3.9
cerebrovascular disease	5.1
ischemic heart disease	6.9
cancer	6.9

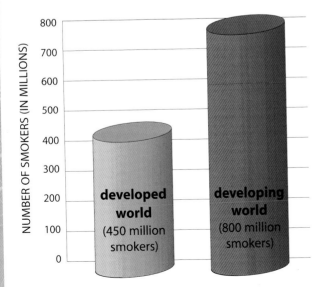

NUMBER OF SMOKERS (IN MILLIONS)

developed world (450 million smokers)

developing world (800 million smokers)

Figure 4: The Smoking Habit (2000)

Tobacco is estimated to cause more than three million deaths each year worldwide, mainly from lung cancer and circulatory diseases. The WHO has warned that tobacco-related diseases will increase dramatically in the future. Although smoking has declined in many developed countries, it is rising in the developing world. Since the link between cancer and smoking was made, the tobacco industry has agreed to pay the United States government billions of dollars over a period of 25 years to cover health care and education costs. However, the U.S. market represents less than five percent of the world market for tobacco products. In Asia, clever advertising and new packaging have persuaded many young people to take up the habit. One-third of those who smoke regularly will die at least 20 years prematurely.

Figure 5: Infection with HIV/AIDS by Region (2000)

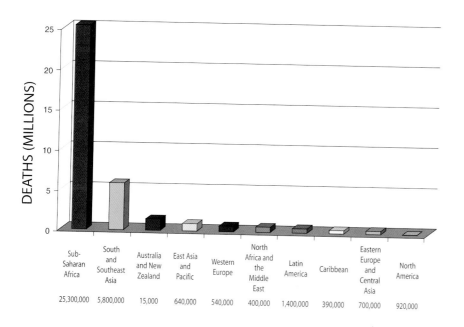

DEATHS (MILLIONS)

Sub-Saharan Africa	South and Southeast Asia	Australia and New Zealand	East Asia and Pacific	Western Europe	North Africa and the Middle East	Latin America	Caribbean	Eastern Europe and Central Asia	North America
25,300,000	5,800,000	15,000	640,000	540,000	400,000	1,400,000	390,000	700,000	920,000

While the world is still without a cure or an effective vaccine against HIV/AIDS, millions of people worldwide are suffering. In 2000, about 36.1 million people were HIV positive, while 5.3 million people were newly infected with the virus. The **pandemic** shows little evidence of slowing down. There were approximately three million AIDS deaths worldwide in 2000. The largest concentration of AIDS sufferers was found in sub-Saharan Africa, where 25.3 million people were living with AIDS.

Figure 6: 20 Years of Living with HIV/AIDS

NUMBER OF PEOPLE LIVING WITH HIV/AIDS (IN MILLIONS)

From the first reported cases of unusual immune system deficiency in the United States to the epidemics in Africa during the 1980s, the number of people worldwide that are affected by HIV/AIDS has increased dramatically during the past 20 years. At least one case of HIV/AIDS has been reported from every region of the world. Global organizations and vaccine trials have not yet been able to control the disease.

1980 '81 '82 '83 '84 '85 '86 '87 '88 '89 '90 '91 '92 '93 '94 '95 '96 '97 '98 '99 2000 2001

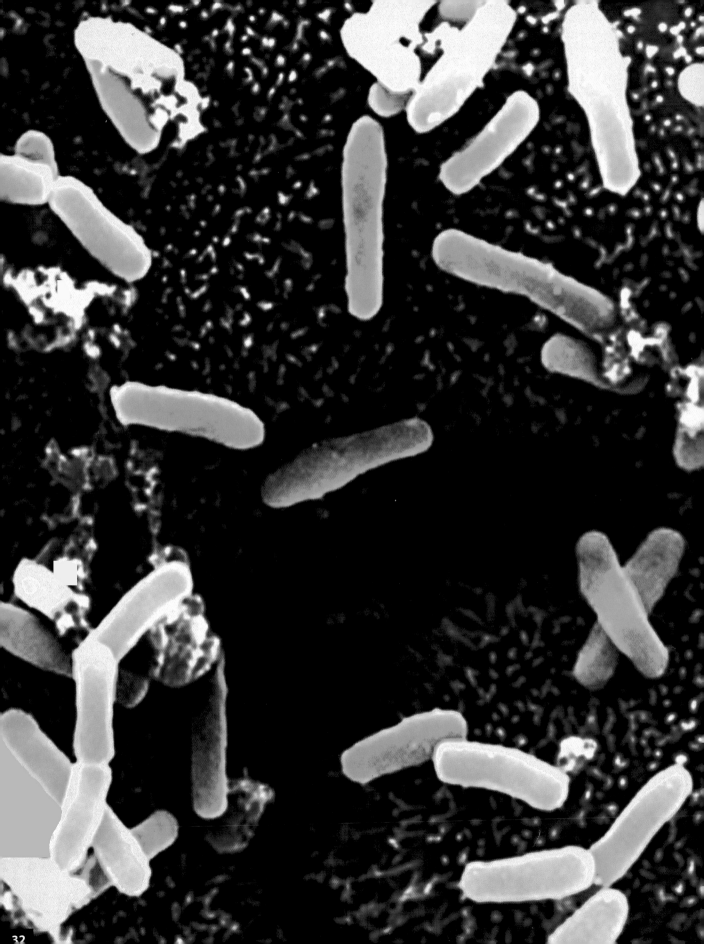

Mortals Versus Microbes

Microbes have evolved alongside people for so long that they are part of the human physical makeup. The line between what is human and what is not has become very hard to draw. Every human being carries billions of microbes. While some of them are harmful, most are helpful or neutral. Microbes live in the intestines, lungs, and on human skin. Invisible to the human eye, they are an essential part of the human system, maintaining balance in the body's systems and internal functions. While humans are unable to live without them, microbes that adapt to a new environment or become resistant to drugs can have disastrous effects on human health.

All sorts of treatments have been used to combat disease. For centuries, bleeding was a common technique used in western medicine, whereby doctors attempted to drain away harmful fluids through induced blood loss. Only during the last century have the physical processes of disease been understood enough for doctors to begin using effective scientific methods. Modern microscopes have allowed today's physicians to see the bacteria and viruses that were undetectable to previous generations of doctors. Still, many modern treatments continue to be based on a combination of knowledge and guesswork.

Every human being carries billions of microbes.

In the 1930s, the use of sulfur-based drugs made a big difference in the treatment of diseases, but their side effects were often very unpleasant. Penicillin, an antibiotic that was discovered accidentally in 1928 by Alexander Fleming, had few harmful side effects and was seen as the new miracle drug. Further antibiotics were discovered, such as streptomycin to treat symptoms of tuberculosis, tetracycline to clear up acne and general infections, and quinolone for urinary tract infections. Thousands of antibiotic products were developed and sold worldwide. Since they were so effective in curing symptoms, courses of antibiotics were often left incomplete, providing ideal conditions for surviving microbes to become resistant to the drugs. When penicillin was first introduced, it could stop most bacterial infections within hours. A four-day treatment of 10,000 units per day would usually cure strep throat. By the mid-1990s, the dose had to be dramatically increased to fight the bacteria that had adapted to penicillin. The required dosage continues to increase today. Repeated doses

Clostridium difficile bacteria, which are present in the intestines of as many as 50 percent of children under age two, can cause serious infections in some cases.

ANTIBIOTIC ABUSE

Many experts warn against the current trend toward overusing and overprescribing antibiotics. Since they became widely available in the 1940s, antibiotic use has rapidly increased:

YEAR		POUNDS PRODUCED IN U.S.
1954		2 million
2000		more than 50 million

of antibiotics may also cause microbial mutations, turning them from harmless passengers into dangerous threats. Microbes can often outsmart the most clever of scientists. The ability of microbes to adapt is astonishing. They have a physical structure that makes them particularly good at adapting to different environments and new conditions. Microbes are becoming increasingly drug resistant. The common bacterium *Staphylococcus aureus*, which penicillin could easily conquer in the 1950s, has become resistant, not only to penicillin, but to most other antibiotics as well. The tendency of microbes to develop resistance demonstrates that they are driven by survival genes. The "superbug" methicillin resistant *Staphylococcus aureus* (MRSA) has become common in hospitals in the developed world. Only one antibiotic, vancomycin, provides hope for humans in the battle against this resilient microbe.

The prospect of hospitals full of people whose wounds will not heal is unpleasant. MRSA seems to be found mostly in hospital environments, where it preys on patients whose immune systems are already weakened. Fortunately, few healthy individuals have been struck down by MRSA. Even the nurses and doctors who work with infected patients do not usually become infected.

Unfortunately, antibiotics can also kill many helpful bacteria along with the harmful

SUPERBUGS

Microbes can reproduce and adapt much more quickly than human beings. A single bacterium may produce a million copies of itself in one day. Sometimes these copies have mutations that provide drug resistance or extra strength. It is very difficult to defend against an enemy whose shape is always changing. As a retrovirus, HIV is able to continuously alter its shape and characteristics. This makes it very difficult to research possible cures. In addition, the virus appears to adapt to individual hosts, so that drugs that work successfully for one patient might not work for another.

Streaks of *Staphylococcus aureus* bacteria treated with the penicillin antibiotic (on the left) demonstrate their resistance to the antibiotic. New derivatives of penicillin applied to bacteria on the right have been developed as a response to bacterial resistance.

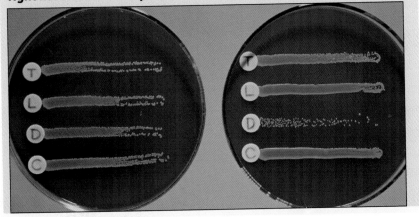

KEY CONCEPTS

Mutation Mutation is change on a cellular level. Such change occurs over time and is the result of environmental factors. Mutation allows organisms to adapt to new circumstances. All organisms have a built-in drive to survive. When humans become infected by a harmful microbe, their bodies resist the invasion. This natural resistance is not always powerful enough to ward off the microbe. As such, drugs are routinely used to combat disease. This practice has advantages and disadvantages.

One obvious advantage of drug therapy is that it enables a person to recover from a particular illness. Not as obvious is the disadvantage that drugs can stimulate mutation in microbes. Many microbial mutations result in increased drug resistance.

A MOUTHFUL OF MICROBES

Perhaps the most worrying use of antibiotics is their routine inclusion in animal feed. More than half the total world production of antibiotics is given to farm animals, either to prevent disease or to promote growth. By consuming milk, eggs, fish, and meat produced from such farm animals, we are gradually reducing the effectiveness of antibiotics in combating serious human infections. The planet's billions of livestock animals, often closely packed in pens, have also increased the number of hosts within which new types of drug-resistant microbes can develop.

Health agencies worldwide, including the WHO, have raised concerns about the use of antibiotics to promote growth in animals.

ones, so the body's natural functions are affected. When diarrhea occurs as a side effect of antibiotic treatment, it is because the digestive system has been damaged by the death of millions of useful microbes in the intestines.

No radical new drugs have been discovered to combat bacteria since 1961. Genetic medicine may eventually provide some relief—although it is unlikely that humans will be able to outsmart all viruses and bacteria. One current area of research is frog venom, which appears to be able to target harmful bacteria, including MRSA, without damaging surrounding human cells. Another possible solution is to change the genetic structure of microbes by deactivating their drug-resistance genes. Genomics, which involves sequencing the genetic code of disease-causing microbes in order to determine new targets for drugs to attack, has been underway for several years now. Experiments in 2000 used high doses of self-assembling molecules to cure particular lethal infections. It could be argued that the attempt to kill all harmful microbes is misguided. Keeping in mind the size and adaptability of the microbial enemy, even genetic solutions may prove hopeless. Some scientists believe that it would be better if humans could somehow use the natural processes of evolution to weaken microbes in a way that would allow mortals and microbes to live safely and naturally side by side.

As a result, drugs must be continually modified in order to maintain their effectiveness.

Genomics The complex science of genomics investigates the structure and function of genes and genetic functions. By genetically engineering plants, genomics has obtained a new understanding of disease resistance and improved nutrients. Genomics can also be applied to the rebuilding of disease cells.

The Age of the Virus

Viruses cause many of the daily illnesses that affect human beings, such as the common cold. They are 20 to 100 times smaller than bacteria. Unlike bacteria, viruses cannot reproduce on their own. Instead, viruses must attach themselves to other cells in order to thrive. Once inside a host cell, they can reproduce and mutate at very high rates. Over centuries, viruses have evolved to develop a symbiotic relationship with many organisms, including human beings. Viruses can attach themselves to human DNA and become linked with the activities of the human body and its organs.

By the time authorities realized that HIV/AIDS was a new type of pandemic, the disease had already taken hold of the population. About 36 million people worldwide were already infected. In 2000, more than three million people around the world died of AIDS. There appear to be two forms of the virus that causes AIDS: HIV-1, which is the version spreading around the world, and HIV-2, a milder form of the disease that occurs mainly in Africa. The origin of HIV-1 has been traced back to chimpanzees, with the first transfer of the virus to a human taking place around 1950. HIV-2 seems to have come from the sooty mangabey monkey. At first limited to a few regions of Africa, HIV-1 was likely brought to the United States by an airline traveler.

Over centuries, viruses have evolved to develop a symbiotic relationship with human beings.

As with many other diseases, including malaria, Africa has been the main victim of AIDS. HIV has affected a large portion of the populations of Kenya, Tanzania, and Malawi, among several other African countries. HIV/AIDS is now sweeping through Asia and Latin America. In the developed world, there is a public perception that HIV is largely under control, as it accounts for only a small proportion of deaths—two percent in the United States—and death rates are falling as new treatments delay the onset of full-blown AIDS. However, AIDS remains incurable, and the number of individuals infected with HIV continues to rise, especially among women. HIV has been a particularly difficult virus to fight. It is a retrovirus, which means that it contains ribonucleic acid (RNA), and the enzyme reverse transcriptase that enables genetic information from viral RNA to become part of the host's DNA. By attacking certain white blood cells, the virus weakens the immune system so that the victim's body cannot defend itself against disease.

So far, the most successful treatment of HIV has been azidothymidine (AZT). This drug confuses HIV by preventing it from copying itself, which stops it from spreading. While

SORRY, THERE IS NO CURE

While scientists have been seeking a cure for the common cold for many years, this virus has proven impossible to defeat. At the same time, there is no cure for HIV/AIDS, which will soon become the biggest killer among current viral diseases. The successful new treatments used in the developed world are too expensive to be used in developing countries, which have 90 percent of the world's HIV cases. HIV/AIDS treatments cost about $20,000 per person, per year. The hope is that a vaccine can be found to combat the virus before it infects the majority of the world's population. So far, results have been disappointing.

This model shows HIV, the virus that causes AIDS. The particles around the outside are proteins that enable HIV to bind and fuse with a target host cell.

DNA-based vaccines may someday protect humans from HIV, the sense of urgency apparent in the 1980s and 1990s, when AIDS was first publicly discussed, has disappeared somewhat.

About 90 percent of all AIDS research is funded by the United States, and research plans are set in motion in response to the country's needs. Today, there is little sign of the large-scale vaccine trials that are needed before mass immunization can begin. Meanwhile, HIV is spreading rapidly through the developing countries of the world, threatening to leave a legacy of orphans and HIV-positive babies.

> *There are viruses that act quickly and with fatal effect.*

The long **incubation period** of AIDS—eight years or more— enables the disease to enter the population before it is even noticed. Other viral diseases, including some cancers, operate in similarly slow and undetected ways. By contrast, there are viruses that act quickly and with fatal effect. While most viral infections produce only mild and temporary symptoms, some can kill within days. The Ebola virus destroys internal tissue, resulting in victims bleeding from their eyes, nose, and mouth. Cases of hantavirus swept across southwestern United States in 1993, killing a dozen people in a particularly unpleasant way—their lungs were drowned in fluid. Hantavirus affects small rodents and can be passed to humans through the inhalation or ingestion of their droppings. It was quickly established that the common deer mouse was the culprit and that the simple act of sweeping the floor, where dry mouse droppings lay, had made the air of family homes lethal to its occupants. At the end of 2001, yellow fever broke out in Ivory Coast, Africa, with fatal results in 21 of the 203 reported cases. Later that year, cases of the disease were reported in Belgium, killing one traveler.

The most horrific diseases tend to die out quickly, partly due to medical responses and partly because they kill so quickly that they run out of hosts. In the 1990s, hemorrhagic fevers, such as dengue fever and the Ebola virus, killed only a few thousand people—through violent fevers, and bleeding—while millions died from more familiar diseases, such as malaria.

SYMBIOSIS

Sometimes species depend on one another to survive. When two different species have a close ecological link to one another, as do HIV and TB, they have a symbiotic relationship. The term symbiosis comes from the Greek word meaning "to live together."

THERE ARE FIVE TYPES OF SYMBIOTIC RELATIONSHIPS:

Mutualism: Both species benefit from the relationship.

Commensalism: One species benefits from the relationship, while the other is unaffected.

Parasitism: One species benefits from the relationship, while the other is harmed.

Competition: Neither species benefits directly from the relationship.

Neutralism: Both species are unaffected by the relationship.

The concern is that since mammals adapt slowly to new conditions, a new airborne virus could have devastating results. After all, more than 90 percent of Australian rabbits were killed when a flea-borne virus was introduced to the country in 1950. Many rabbits have since developed immunity. Humankind, with its slow reproduction and complex civilization, would require centuries to recover from a pandemic of this scale.

KEY CONCEPTS

Incubation HIV is known for its long incubation period. A person could potentially remain healthy for years after becoming infected with the virus. While science has yet to give the world a cure for HIV/AIDS, there is some hope that it can control the disease. Researchers at Emory University in Atlanta, Georgia, are waiting for Godot, a rhesus monkey that has remained healthy despite having been infected with HIV. Godot is the focus of a study that is testing a vaccine against HIV. While the vaccine does not stop HIV from entering the body, it has stopped the disease from taking hold in Godot. By the end of 2001, reports remained promising as Godot was still healthy. If the vaccine is able to extend the incubation period of HIV, it could become extremely valuable in the fight against the spread of the disease.

Pharmacist

Duties: Prepares and dispenses drugs, which help in the treatment of disease
Education: Bachelor of science degree in pharmacy
Interests: Public health, chemistry, medicine, and interacting with people

Navigate to the American Public Health Association Web site: www.apha.org/ for information on related careers. Also, click on www.pharmacistjobs.com/ for more information about pharmacy jobs.

Careers in Focus

The daily tasks of a pharmacist include the **compounding** and dispensing of drugs, and the provision of drug-related information to customers. A pharmacist is an expert on medical treatments and the therapeutic value of medicines or drugs. Responsible for pointing out safety precautions—including whether particular antibiotics must be taken with food, react poorly with other medications, or have side effects, such as drowsiness or nausea—the pharmacist helps people suffering from disease combat their symptoms by explaining how to effectively administer medical treatments. The goals of the pharmacist are primarily to cure disease, eliminate or reduce symptoms of disease, slow the progress of disease, and to prevent disease.

Pharmacists serve the community by providing information and advice on the best ways in which to use medicines and drugs, and alternative ways to combat symptoms and diseases. Using computer technology, pharmacists today are able to maintain and monitor patient records. By combining information about the patient with news about advances in drugs and new medical technologies, the pharmacist can help those suffering from disease to live active, normal lives.

In essence, the pharmacist is concerned with improving the quality of life of the people in a community by helping prevent, treat, and cure diseases and by educating a population on the benefits and advantages of medical treatment.

The Goal of Health for All

When the World Health Organization (WHO) was set up in 1946, its goal was to enable everyone in the world to attain the highest possible level of health. Health was defined as "a state of complete physical, mental, and social well-being." In 1977, the target of "Health for All by the Year 2000" was set. Unfortunately, the goal was not

> **The target of "Health for All by the Year 2000" was not achieved.**

achieved. This is not, however, because the medical profession has been unable to meet the challenge. Despite the limits of science in disease control and treatment, modern medicine has been able to protect most people—at least in industrialized countries—from the daily risks of sudden illness and death. The fact that the health care standards of Switzerland have not been achieved in every country cannot be blamed on doctors or health care professionals. Although doctors have clearly identified the steps necessary to maintain good health, many people choose to disregard their instructions. People still smoke, abuse drugs, live inactive lifestyles, and eat unhealthy foods. At the same

Education and medicine are important to well-being. India's schools are striving to provide their students with regular medical checkups.

THE HEALTHIEST COUNTRIES

The WHO's annual report in 2000 assessed the world's health-care systems. The analysis used the following indicators to measure the health-care systems of 191 member states: an index of population health, health inequalities within the population, the level of health system responsiveness, the distribution of responsiveness within the population, and the distribution of the health system's financial burden within the population. While the United States spends a higher proportion of its gross domestic product (GDP) on health care than any other country in the world, the report found that it ranked only 37th out of the 191 countries in health performance. The United Kingdom, which spends just six percent of its GDP on health services, ranked 18th. The report concluded that France provides the best overall health care, followed by countries such as Italy, Spain, Austria, and Japan. Some small countries, generally thought to be incapable of supporting successful health-care systems, rank close behind second-place Italy: San Marino, Andorra, Malta, and Singapore. The report indicates that there exist wide variations in health-care provisions, even between countries having similar health-care systems and spending policies. This means that many countries are not adequately using their resources. Using this report as a guide, the WHO plans to assist policy makers in redistributing health system resources to more effectively reach the goal of global health.

time, poverty plays a major role in health as well. While wealth is no guarantee of good health, poverty is almost always accompanied by sickness. The least developed countries tend to have the greatest incidence of disease. Thus, health for all depends on more than just medicine for its achievement.

Health for all is something that can only be achieved with major changes in politics, economics, and human behavior across the planet. Less ambitious goals, such as the eradication of polio, measles, and leprosy, seem within reach, and are very important first steps.

The WHO provides annual reports on the state of world health. It needs the support of other international bodies to bring about change. Organizations, such as the United Nations Development Programme (UNDP), the World Bank, and the World Trade Organization, could help heal the world by devising better ways to distribute wealth. They could also help provide the basic building blocks for long-term health—clean water, sanitation, nutritious food, and education.

Health for all depends on more than just medicine.

A more basic requirement is peace, since war is often accompanied by outbreaks of disease. Thus, "health for all" cannot be achieved without universal peace, political stability, and economic development. While this ideal world seems beyond reach, many organizations continue to work toward such a goal. Doctors provide much hope for the world, and they can often cross barriers that keep politicians out. Even in a world ravaged by war and suffering, it has been possible to immunize 80 percent of the planet's children against 6 of the most common killer diseases. In India, in 1997, more than 130 million children were immunized against polio in just one single day. In a country where political differences often delay action, it is hard to imagine any other project that would have received such widespread support.

There is no doubt that new health risks have emerged as a result of modern lifestyles. Since the recycling of cabin air was introduced as a fuel-saving measure in the 1980s, even breathing the air in airplanes has become a health risk. Disease is too clever and too complex to be defeated entirely. Conditions such as asthma and diabetes have replaced diseases such as scarlet fever and smallpox. There are some experts who are even beginning to question the wisdom of mass vaccinations and the widespread use of medical drugs. They argue that the overuse of drugs prompts too many mutations in disease. These mutations lower the effectiveness of the human immune system.

Even before the discovery of sulfur-based drugs and penicillin, certain infectious diseases were close to being defeated. This was a result of improved nutrition, cleaner water, and more hygienic living conditions in the developed world. Clearly, there is no single answer to the world's health problems. Action must be taken in a number of ways. It is up to society, as a whole, to deal with such issues as social justice, education, and community development— all of which have major effects on human health.

Only recently has there been a serious attempt to monitor emerging or reemerging diseases. Though fast-acting diseases always make the news, some scientists are beginning to question the health effects of environmental damage, such as **ozone** depletion's links to cancers, and the new chemical compounds that are seeping into the world's food, water, and air, causing respiratory and digestive disorders. Their questions are helping to shift the concerns of the global population.

In the long term, the mixing of the world's population should provide a stronger **gene pool** and therefore improved immune systems. New medical techniques and increased levels of education around the world provide the planet's best hopes for a healthy future. However, humans have to recognize that disease cannot be completely defeated. The best hope is in its management and control.

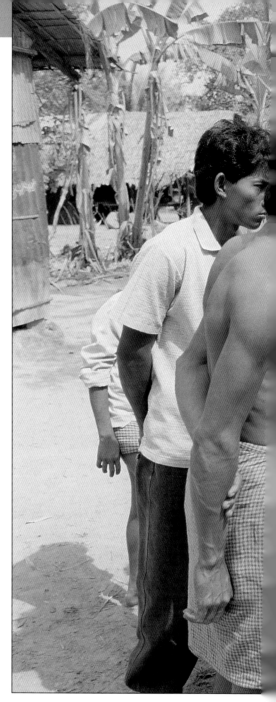

Water development projects, such as this one in Cambodia, are a vital step toward providing worldwide "health for all."

KEY CONCEPTS

War In order for people to attain the highest possible level of health, there first has to be peace in their country. War has a serious effect on the stability of a nation. When a country is at war, its economic resources are strained. Government funds used for weapons and soldiers are drastically increased. As a result, certain key services are affected. New hospitals are not built during wars, nor are new schools. Sometimes, existing ones are forced to shut down. This makes it very difficult for citizens to access the services and knowledge they require to remain healthy.

Access While treatments are available for many diseases, access to them depends on several factors, including politics and economics. The cost of medication is often too great for many of the world's citizens. Pharmaceutical corporations are responsible for developing the

drugs needed to treat the world's diseases. Developing these drugs is very costly, and much of the cost is passed on to the consumer. In developed countries, most drugs are affordable to those who need them. In developing countries, the opposite is often the case.

Most residents of the United States can afford to pay $50 for a necessary drug treatment. That same $50 may take months for a citizen in Mali to earn. While the pharmaceutical companies are in the business of helping people, they are still in business. Their costs must be recoverable

if they hope to compete in the marketplace. Despite the efforts of the World Health Organization, global medical effort is heavily weighted toward helping the world's wealthier patients.

Dictionary of Diseases

DISEASE	SYMPTOMS, CAUSES, AND TRANSFER
AIDS	weakened immune system, increased sensitivity to infections; transmitted through blood or blood products that enter the body's bloodstream; caused by HIV
Alzheimer's disease	dementia, loss of memory, mental deterioration; unknown cause, but takes effect in late middle age; nontransferable
anthrax	from skin infection to common cold-like symptoms to abdominal pain, vomiting of blood and severe diarrhea; transmitted through sheep and cattle, in which it naturally occurs, or by inhalation of the spores
arthritis	painful inflammation of the body's joints; caused by gradual bone deterioration; nontransferable
asthma	bronchial contractions, wheezing, and difficulty breathing; often triggered by allergic reactions; nontransferable
bubonic plague	severe infection; formation of inflammatory swellings of lymphatic glands, called buboes, at the armpits and groin; transmitted through rodent bites or fleas that carry the bacterium
cancer	invasive growths or tumors in the body; often caused by environmental factors and hereditary characteristics; nontransferable
Chagas disease	from no symptoms to swelling of the eye on one side of the face to cardiac problems; caused by a protozoan parasite transmitted by blood-sucking insects
cholera	severe infection of the small intestine; causes severe diarrhea and dehydration; transmitted in contaminated drinking water; caused by bacteria
common cold	sneezing, coughing, sore throat; since not highly contagious, must have close, prolonged contact for transmission, caused by more than 200 viruses
dengue fever	violent fever, severe pains in the joints and muscles; found in warm climates, and usually emerges in epidemic proportions from four closely related viruses
depression	prolonged emotional dejection, sadness, and withdrawal from social engagement; influenced by social and/or environmental factors, genetics, or biology; nontransferable
diabetes	unusually high levels of glucose in the blood, increased urination; may be related to diet, but is often hereditary; nontransferable
diphtheria	fever, weakness, and the formation of a false membrane in air passages, especially severe inflammation of throat; caused by bacteria
Ebola virus	hemorrhagic fever, gastrointestinal distress, and death; caused by contact with a reservoir host, an animal, or anthropod involved in the life cycle of the virus
elephantiasis	enlargement of the legs, scrotum, and other body parts; due to obstruction of the lymphatic vessels by an infestation of parasitic worms in the blood
emphysema	difficulty breathing, abnormal enlargement and loss of elasticity of air spaces; often caused by smoking or environmental pollution; nontransferable
encephalitis	inflammation of the substance of the brain; viral infection transmitted by mosquitoes

E. coli	diarrhea and abdominal cramps; transmitted by eating undercooked, contaminated ground beef containing the bacteria
hantavirus	severe respiratory disorders, kidney failure, among other symptoms; virus is spread by wild rodents
HIV	invades and inactivates immune system functions, results in AIDS; virus is transmitted through blood or blood products that enter the body's bloodstream
influenza	weakness, exhaustion, cold-like symptoms, fever, and vomiting; often in epidemic proportions; its viruses are airborne
legionnaires' disease	affects the respiratory system; acquired by inhaling airborne droplets from contaminated water supplies containing the bacteria
leprosy	destruction of tissue, loss of sensation, skin inflammation; slightly infectious; bacteria is spread mainly through nose droplets
Lyme disease	joint pains, fatigue, and sometimes neurological disorders; caused by bacteria living in the fur of wild deer; transferred by ticks
malaria	attacks of chills, fevers, and sweating; parasites are transferred to the human bloodstream by mosquitoes
measles	small red spots on the skin, fever, and cold-like symptoms; usually occurring in childhood, virus is transferred through direct contact with nose or throat secretions
MRSA	from no symptoms to tenderness, swelling, and redness at the site of the infection; transferred by *Staphylococcus aureus* bacteria resistant to methicillin that get inside the body and cause infection
polio	affects motor nerves, often destroying muscle functions and causing skeletal deformity; formerly epidemic in children and young adults, virus is now controlled by vaccination
Rift Valley Fever	no symptoms or mild illness associated with fever and liver abnormalities; virus is transmitted by mosquito bites, or exposure to blood and other body fluids of infected animals
river blindness	serious visual impairment, rashes, lesions, itching, and depigmentation of the skin; caused by an infestation of parasitic worms
scarlet fever	fever, appearance of a red rash; caused by Group A *hemolytic streptococci* (same bacteria that cause strep throat); transmitted through direct contact
schizophrenia	disorganized speech and behavior, delusions, and hallucinations; associated with brain abnormalities; nontransferable
smallpox	acute fever, pustular eruptions that leave pits or scars in the skin; highly contagious, virus has been eradicated through worldwide vaccination programs
tetanus	spasms and muscle rigidity, especially of the lower jaw and neck; the bacteria commonly enter the body through a wound or cut by rusty metals
tuberculosis	affects any tissue in the body, but especially the lungs, swelling and lesions can appear on bone or the surface of the body; spread by airborne bacteria in coughs and sneezes
typhus	acute weakness and exhaustion, headache, and reddish spots; bacteria transmitted by lice and fleas
whooping cough	a series of short, convulsive coughs, followed by an immense intake of breath; infects the membranes in the respiratory system; caused by the bacterium *Bordetella pertussis*
yellow fever	acute, often fatal, fever; characterized by liver damage and jaundice; virus is transmitted by mosquitoes in warm climates

Time Line of Events

430 B.C.
A plague hits Athens, Greece, and spreads to Sparta. Lasting two years, it kills nearly one-third of the population.

A.D. 542
A plague hits Constantinople (now Istanbul, Turkey). Spreading rapidly, on some days the daily death toll reaches close to 10,000 people.

1347–1350
Bubonic plague devastates Europe. More than one-third of the population dies.

1388
The city of Cambridge, England, passes the first sanitation laws in Europe.

1492
While exploring North America, Christopher Columbus introduces smallpox, TB, and influenza to the Native-American population. Without immunity to these new diseases, several million people die.

1796
Edward Jenner discovers the principle of vaccination—that injection with a minute dose of a disease can provide lifelong immunity against its full-blown form.

1865
Surgeon Joseph Lister uses carbolic acid to sanitize an operation site.

1877
Louis Pasteur develops a vaccine against anthrax.

1883
The cholera microbe is discovered by Robert Koch.

1908
The polio virus is discovered. It was previously believed to be a bacterium.

1918–1920
A major influenza outbreak kills almost 20 million people around the world.

1928
Alexander Fleming discovers penicillin.

1933
Yellow fever outbreak is recorded in Brazil and Colombia.

1946
The World Health Organization is established. Its constitution is approved and signed by the 61 nations represented.

ca. 1950
The first HIV transfer to humans occurs.

1954
Jonas Salk's polio vaccine proves effective.

1955
The average human life expectancy is 48 years.

1969
The first known case of HIV is discovered—years after the victim's death—in the U.S.

1972
Biological weapons are outlawed.

1976
The Ebola virus is identified in the Democratic Republic of the Congo.

1977

Smallpox is eradicated worldwide.

1979

The last case of polio is reported in the United States.

1981

AIDS is identified.

1991

A major cholera outbreak occurs in Peru—the first in more than a century.

1992

A major cholera outbreak occurs in India.

1993

The WHO declares a global TB emergency.

1994

The U.S. reports 441,528 cases of AIDS.

1994

A bubonic plague outbreak devastates India.

1995

The average human life expectancy is 65 years.

1996

The World Health Organization's annual report focuses on infectious diseases.

1997

The World Health Organization's annual report focuses on chronic diseases.

1997

About 130 million children in India are vaccinated against polio.

1997

More than 2.3 million people worldwide die from AIDS.

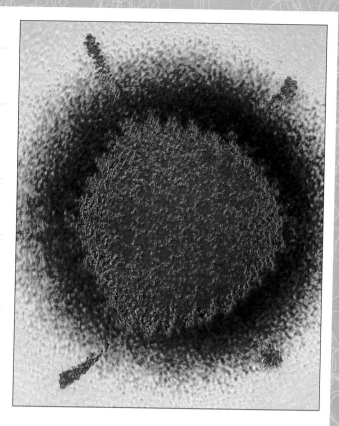

Despite its many achievements throughout history, medicine has yet to find a cure for the common cold. However, scientists are close to discovering how the virus uses its receptors (shown above, along the outer edges, in red) to gain entry into a host cell.

1997

The *Staphylococcus aureus* bacterium, or Golden Staph, is discovered to be resistant to the last line of antibiotic defense, vancomycin.

2000

The World Health Organization's annual report focuses on mental disorders.

2001

During the months following terrorist attacks on New York City's World Trade Center and Virginia's Pentagon, several cases of bioterrorism-related anthrax are reported in the United States.

Concept Web

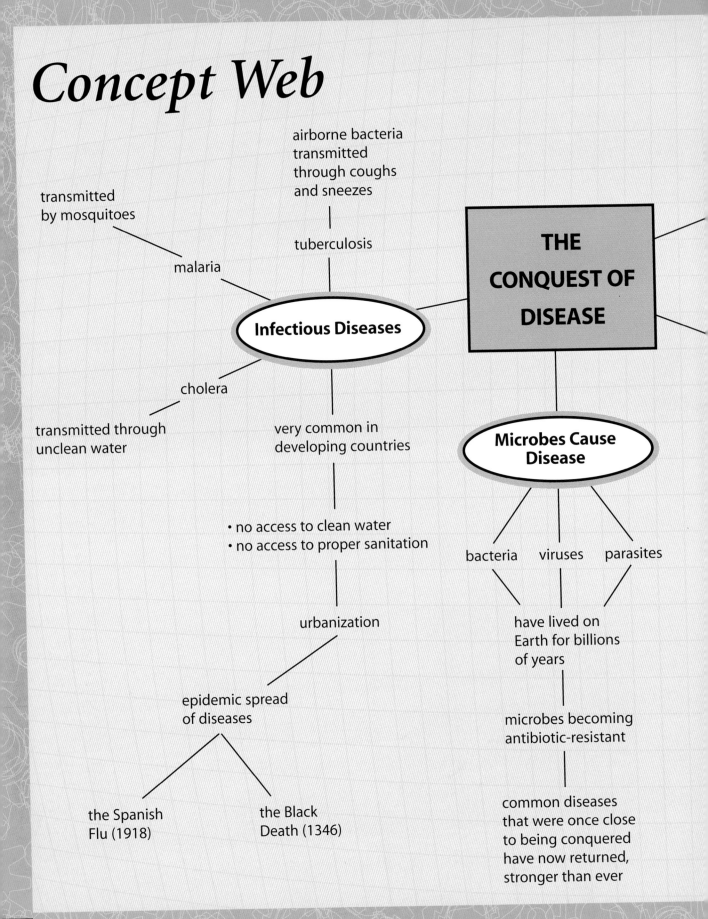

airborne bacteria transmitted through coughs and sneezes

tuberculosis

transmitted by mosquitoes

malaria

THE CONQUEST OF DISEASE

Infectious Diseases

cholera

transmitted through unclean water

very common in developing countries

Microbes Cause Disease

• no access to clean water
• no access to proper sanitation

bacteria   viruses   parasites

have lived on Earth for billions of years

urbanization

microbes becoming antibiotic-resistant

epidemic spread of diseases

the Spanish Flu (1918)

the Black Death (1346)

common diseases that were once close to being conquered have now returned, stronger than ever

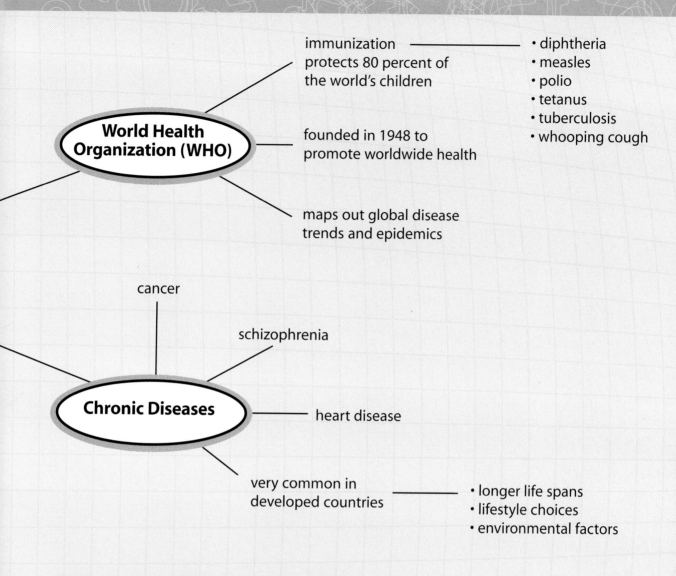

immunization —————— • diphtheria
protects 80 percent of • measles
the world's children • polio
• tetanus
World Health • tuberculosis
Organization (WHO) founded in 1948 to • whooping cough
promote worldwide health

maps out global disease
trends and epidemics

cancer

schizophrenia

Chronic Diseases

heart disease

very common in —————— • longer life spans
developed countries • lifestyle choices
• environmental factors

MAKE YOUR OWN CONCEPT WEB

A concept web is a useful summary tool. It can also be used to plan your research or help you write an essay or report. To make your own concept web, follow the steps below:

- You will need a large piece of unlined paper and a pencil.
- First, read through your source material, such as *The Conquest of Disease* in the Understanding Global Issues series.
- Write the main idea, or concept, in large letters in the center of the page.
- On a sheet of lined paper, jot down all words, phrases, or lists that you know are connected with the concept. Try to do this from memory.
- Look at your list. Can you group your words and phrases in certain topics or themes? Connect the different topics with lines to the center, or to other "branches."
- Critique your concept web. Ask questions about the material on your concept web: Does it all make sense? Are all the links shown? Could there be other ways of looking at it? Is anything missing?
- What more do you need to find out? Develop questions for those areas you are still unsure about or where information is missing. Use these questions as a basis for further research.

Quiz

Milestones
Match the medical researchers with their disease milestones.

1. Louis Pasteur
2. Alexander Fleming
3. Robert Koch
4. Jonas Salk

a) convinced doctors of the existence of disease-carrying germs.
b) developed the polio vaccine.
c) discovered penicillin.
d) developed the anthrax vaccine.

Diagnosis
From the symptoms or the transmission methods listed, determine the following diseases.

1. degeneration of the brain
2. transmitted through contact with contaminated blood
3. transmitted via the *Anopheles* mosquito
4. soaring body temperature, pain, confusion, and if left untreated, death in two to three days
5. caused by bacteria in the fur of wild deer, and transmitted through tick bites

a) bubonic plague
b) Alzheimer's disease
c) Lyme disease
d) HIV/AIDS
e) malaria

True or False

1. Microbes can adapt very quickly to new environments.
2. Only humans are affected by disease.
3. Global warming could increase the incidence of malaria.
4. Everyone in the world has access to medical treatment.
5. Diseases can become resistant to drugs.

Multiple Choice

1. The Black Death
    a) killed close to one-third of Europe's population.
    b) caused 20 million people to die between 1346 and 1350.
    c) was an infectious disease.
    d) all of the above.

2. Chronic diseases
    a) are infectious.
    b) affect only developing countries.
    c) can be caused by infectious viruses or bacteria, lifestyle behaviors, and environmental pollution.
    d) all of the above.

3. Immunization
    a) treats the symptoms of a disease.
    b) controls the spread of disease within a population, by initiating the body's immunity to it.
    c) eradicates a disease.
    d) all of the above.

4. A virus
    a) can reproduce on its own.
    b) requires a host cell in order to reproduce.
    c) can be treated with antibiotics.
    d) all of the above.

5. The World Health Organization
    a) wants everyone in the world to achieve the highest level of health possible.
    b) declared a global tuberculosis emergency in 1993.
    c) was founded in 1946.
    d) all of the above.

Answers on page 53

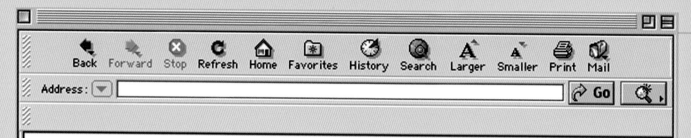

Internet Resources

The following are international organizations involved in the battle against disease:

WHO

<u>**http://www.who.int/home-page**</u>

Since its establishment in 1946, the World Health Organization (WHO) has attempted to aid individuals, in every country of the world, obtain the goal of health. From the creation of immunization programs to the upgrading of the developing world's water supplies, the WHO has been an important force in the quest to conquer global disease. The WHO Web site is a clear, informative source for topics such as recent disease outbreaks, disease prevention, and symptoms of certain diseases to watch out for. Individuals can search the archives for news articles and reports, including the annual World Health Reports.

CDC

<u>**http://www.cdc.gov**</u>

Search disease topics alphabetically, read up on current disease trends, outbreaks, and treatments, access various medical publications and links, and find out about the Centers for Disease Control and Prevention, the leading federal agency for protecting health and safety in the United States.

Some Web sites stay current longer than others. To find other disease Web sites, enter terms such as "infectious disease," "immunization," or "virus" into a search engine.

Further Reading

Dudley Gold, Susan. *Alzheimer's Disease, Revised Edition.* Berkeley Heights: Enslow Publishers Inc., 2001.

Farrell, Jeanette. *Invisible Enemies: Stories of Infectious Disease.* New York: Farrar, Straus & Giroux, 1998.

Greenberg, Alissa. *Asthma.* New York: Franklin Watts, Inc., 2000.

Manning, Karen. *AIDS: Can This Epidemic Be Stopped (Issues for our Time).* Breckenridge: Twenty First Century Books, 1995.

Nardo, Don. (ed.) *The Black Death.* San Diego: Greenhaven Press, 1999.

Yount, Lisa. *Epidemics.* San Diego: Lucent Books, 2000.

World Health Organization, World Health Reports:
1996: Fighting Disease, Fostering Development
1997: Conquering Suffering, Enriching Humanity
1998: Life in the 21ˢᵗ Century: A Vision for All
1999: Making a Difference
2000: Health Systems: Improving Performance
2001: Mental Health: New Understanding, New Hope

Answers

Milestones
1. d) 2. c) 3. a) 4. b)

Diagnosis
1. b) 2. d) 3. e) 4. a) 5. c)

True or False
1. T 2. F 3. T 4. F 5. T

Multiple Choice
1. d) 2. c) 3. b) 4. b) 5. d)

Glossary

bacteria: microscopic single-celled organisms involved in infectious diseases

compounding: producing medicines by combining two or more ingredients

conquistadors: early Spanish conquerors of the Americas, especially Peru and Mexico

debilitating: weakening

deoxyribonucleic acid (DNA): a self-replicating nucleic acid that carries genetic information

evolution: the gradual development of a species or group of organisms

fermentation: a chemical change brought about by a ferment, such as yeast enzymes in the process of converting grape sugar into alcohol

gene pool: the total genetic information of all the individuals in a population

genes: the basic physical units that transmit hereditary characteristics

germs: disease-producing microorganisms

globalization: the movement of people, goods, and money to become a worldwide system

hosts: living animals or plants from which a parasite obtains its nutrients

immune system: the complex system by which the body defends itself against disease

incubation period: the time between the initial infection and the first appearance of symptoms of a disease

Industrial Revolution: a time period when machines altered the way people worked and lived in many parts of the world

lymphatic system: the network of ducts that transports fluids and aids the body in the fight against disease

microbes: microorganisms, especially disease-causing bacteria

mood disorders: diseases that affect a person's emotional state

mutate: to alter an individual or species by changing a gene or chromosome

nervous system disorders: diseases that affect a person's brain, spinal cord, or nerves

ozone: the form of oxygen that absorbs ultraviolet rays in the upper atmosphere, preventing them from reaching Earth's surface

pandemic: a disease that spreads throughout an entire country, continent, or the world

parasites: organisms living on or within hosts, from which they obtain their nutrients

pasteurization: the process of destroying harmful microorganisms in liquids, such as milk, by heating them

transfusions: direct transfers of blood or plasma into blood vessels

viruses: microscopic infectious agents that copy themselves only within the cells of living hosts

Index

Index

Photo Credits

Cover: Ebola virus (**Scott Camazine**); **Title Page:** Surgery (**Kindra Clineff Photography**); **Lester V. Bergman/CORBIS/MAGMA:** page 34; **Biozentrum, Science Photo Library:** page 47; **Scott Camazine:** pages 2/3, 4, 6, 19, 20, 26; **Jean-Loup Charmet, Science Photo Library:** page 8; **DigitalVision:** page 25m; **EyeWire Inc.:** pages 14, 24, 27; **Mike Grandmaison:** page 35; **Jim King/Photo Agora:** page 43; **Kindra Clineff Photography:** pages 10, 13, 15, 39; **PhotoDisc:** page 25t; **Noah Poritz, Science Photo Library:** page 25b; **Saskatchewan Archives Board:** page 7; **Harmit Singh/World Bank Photo Library:** page 40; **The Wellcome Trust: Audio Visual, LHSTM/Wellcome Trust Photo Library:** page 17; **Jan Hobot/Wellcome Photo Library:** page 32; **K. Hodivala-Dilke, M. Stone/Wellcome Photo Library:** page 23; **National Medical Slide Bank/Wellcome Photo Library:** page 12; **Wellcome Photo Library:** pages 18, 21, 22; **John Wildgoose/Wellcome Trust Photo Library:** page 37; **Rob Young/Wellcome Photo Library:** page 9.